conspiracy

conspiracy

HISTORY"S GREATEST PLOTS, COLLUSIONS AND COVER-UPS

Charlotte Greig

BARNES & NOBLE

NEW YORK

© 2003 by Arcturus Publishing Limited

This 2006 edition published by Barnes & Noble Publishing, Inc. by
arrangement with Arcturus Publishing Limited

Editor: Paul Whittle
Design: Talking Design
Cover Design: Steve Flight
Cover images: Corbis

2006 Barnes & Noble Publishing

ISBN-13: 978-0-7607-8489-1
ISBN-10: 0-7607-8489-2

Printed and bound in China

10 9 8 7 6 5 4 3 2 1

Contents

INTROD

POST 9/11 WE ARE IN A GOLDEN AGE OF THE
CONSPIRACY THEORY. THE SUCCESS OF MICHAEL
MOORE'S FAHRENHEIT 911 HAS MADE THIS KIND OF
ALTERNATIVE HISTORY POSITIVELY RESPECTABLE:
NOWADAYS, IT'S NOT JUST CRAZED LONERS WHO SPEND
TOO MUCH TIME ON THE INTERNET DISCUSSING WHY
GEORGE BUSH CARRIED ON READING A CHILDREN'S
STORY AFTER BEING TOLD THE FIRST PLANE HAD HIT THE
WORLD TRADE CENTRE, OR SCANNING THE BUSINESS
PAGES TO FIND OUT WHETHER THE 'WAR ON TERROR' IS
REALLY THE WAR FOR MORE OIL.

Often enough, yesterday's conspiracy theory is today's accepted history. If you'd said at the time that Hitler started the Reichstag Fire himself to smear his Communist opposition you'd have be called paranoid. Now it's an accepted fact. And how many people today really believe that JFK was assassinated by Lee Harvey Oswald acting all alone? And are we wrong to see conspiracies in the links between, say, the US government and Halliburton or Enron? Or naïve not to?

Of course, not all conspiracy theories have a basis in fact. Some are outlandish, such as the theory that that the world is hollow and inhabited at the centre; others, such as the notion that the government is hushing up alien visitations here, there and everywhere, seem like the stuff of X files episodes. Yet all of them, even the most bizarre, address facts that cannot easily be explained, or point to our psychological need to find a reason for everything that takes place in our world.

Then there are those conspiracy theories that hover entertainingly on the edge of possibility: for example, the idea that the moon landings were faked up in a film studio. And, of course, there's not a celebrity death without its attendant conspiracy theory. Was Princess Diana murdered? Is Elvis still alive? Was the FBI really behind John Lennon's murder? To some, these theories simply demonstrate

UCTION

our human tendency to deny death and loss, to let our idols go; to others, they reveal the sinister currents of money and power that run below the public life of any celebrated figure in our culture today.

This book gathers together more than forty of the most compelling conspiracies: ranging from the genuinely credible to the frankly implausible, from paedophile conspiracies to crop circles, from Watergate to the Holy Grail. Was Pearl Harbour a set-up? Was Marilyn Monroe murdered? We may not have the answers, but we've got some pretty good theories!

What is a Conspiracy Theory?

The words conspiracy comes form the Latin conspirare. Literally it means 'to breathe together'. In practice it refers to two or more people making a plan of action. Theoretically that plan could be either good or bad, but over the centuries

it has gained a distinctly negative sense. You can see this clearly from the way in which the word is used in the legal sphere: 'conspiracy' in a legal sense always refers to wrongdoing.

Conspiracies are not by definition secret but as the word has attached itself to criminal behaviour that's almost inevitably a part of the package. So, over the years, secrecy has become a part of our conventional sense of what a conspiracy is. And it's a crucial part when it comes to the development of conspiracy theories. Essentially, conspiracy theories are alternative explanations of history or of the world about us. Conspiracy theories suggest that dramatic events happen not by accident or for apparent reasons, but because of plans made in secrecy.

There's no doubt that conspiracy theories have been with us for thousands of years. After al conspiracies certainly

CONSPIRACY THEORIES SUGGEST THAT DRAMATIC EVENTS HAPPEN NOT BY ACCIDENT, BUT BECAUSE OF PLANS MADE IN SECRECY.

INTROD

UCTION

have. Whether it's the ancient Greeks conspiring to take over Troy or the Caesar's rivals conspiring to assassinate him, history is full of dramatic conspiracies. And there have always been people with a suspicious cast of mind who've come up with conspiracy theories to explain such events.

However, it's only in the past hundred years or so that conspiracy theories have really come to the fore. Perhaps that has something to do with the decline of religion. In the past people tended to see inexplicable events as the work of the Almighty. In our more secular times, however, people tend to look for the nefarious hand of man.

The late nineteenth century saw the birth of some enduring conspiracy theories. As the world was changing fast through industrialisation, and the old certainties of life were being shattered, many people started to suspect that there was some powerful organisation controlling all this, some group who were effectively setting themselves up as rivals to God. The prime candidates for this role, in a Europe in which anti-Semitism had long been rife, were the Jewish communities. The idea of an international Jewish conspiracy began to gain credence, especially in Russia in the turbulent years leading up to the first world war. Other candidates for the role of secret rulers of the world included the Freemasons, the Communists, and the semi-mythical group known as the Illuminati.

Such visions of a world controlled by a small and sinister cabal are still a popular element in conspiracy theoriestoday. In fact they lie behind almost every conspiracy theory there is. So perhaps the answer to the question 'what is a conspiracy theory?' should be 'it's a theory which suggests that the great world

OTHER CANDIDATES FOR THE ROLE OF SECRET RULERS OF THE WORLD INCLUDE THE FREEMASONS, THE COMMUNISTS, AND THE ILLUMINATI.

INTROD

events are not what they seem; rather, they are the manifestations of a world controlled by a secret elite.'

CONSPIRACY THEORIES TODAY

There has been an explosion of interest in conspiracy theories in recent years. There are many possible reasons for this - loss of faith in religion, as mentioned above, loss of faith in politicians, a sensationalist mass media that likes to broadcast sensational theories, the influence of films and novels espousing conspiracies, and so on. One major factor is undoubtedly the growth of the internet. The internet is the perfect medium for spreading conspiracy theories. Where once a rumour would be passed around a chosen few insiders and spread slowly through the metropolitan grapevine – for example, the rumour about the identity of the masked man at the London sex parties at the heart of the Profumo affair, or the one about the identity of the Watergate source known as 'Deep Throat' – these days, it will be on the internet in minutes and instantly transmitted around the world.

Thus today, when a major event occurs – take 9/11 for example – conspiracy theories immediately start to circulate on the internet. Evidence that the authorities would prefer to have kept quiet is now available to be discussed and interpreted from America to Australia. The trouble is, of course, that so too are lies, fabrications and delusions. The internet is at once a marvellous tool for avoiding censorship and allowing the voice of truth to emerge, and also a forum in which every lunatic and partisan commentator can have their say. Today, when so many conspiracy theories appear on the internet, it is sometimes a difficult business to determine which ones are worthy of

WHEN A MAJOR EVENT OCCURS – 9/11 FOR EXAMPLE – CONSPIRACY THEORIES IMMEDIATELY START TO CIRCULATE ON THE INTERNET.

UCTION

serious consideration and which are simply hearsay.

This dilemma has never been clearer that when dealing with the events of 9/1l and the subsequent war on terror. The extraordinary success of Michael Moore's documentary film *Fahrenheit 911* has seen conspiracy theories go mainstream. The film takes seriously a number of conspiracy theories that might previously have been thought outlandish. As a result, audiences have been polarised. Some see the film as irresponsible, others see it as uttering the truths that the regular news media was scared to utter. Ultimatel,y their responses tended to depend on what side of the political fence the viewer happened to be sitting on. This is hardly surprising: conspiracy theories always tend to appeal to those whose political views are in opposition to those in power.

POLITICAL CONSPIRACIES

This book will attempt to offer an unbiased investigation into several aspects of the war on terror and leave the reader to make up their own mind. We'll explore the various conspiracy theories relating to the events of 9/11 itself. We'll try to make sense of the mysterious last moments of

Flight 93, the plane brought down by its passengers. We'll look into the accusation that the war on Afghanistan was a war on oil and we'll investigate the tangled links between the Bush family and the Bin Ladens.

Political conspiracy theories are nothing new, of course. So we'll also look into some the classic political mysteries of yesteryear. We'll investigate the sinking of the *Lusitania* asking who really sank the ocean liner – the event that persuaded the USA to join in World War One. And what about Pearl Harbor ? Did Roosevelt really let it happen in order to persuade Americans to join in World War Two? We'll look into one of the most long-running and pernicious of all conspiracy theories as we explore just why people want to deny that the Holocaust ever happened. And on a slightly lighter note, we'll look into whether Adolf Hitler could really have escaped the bunker by a secret tunnel and fled to Antarctica with Eva Braun.

Coming closer to the present, we'll examine at the string of suspicious deaths and assassinations that occurred during the 1960s. The most celebrated of these, the murder of JFK, is perhaps the ultimate conspiracy theory, with endless books,

INTROD

COULD THE POPE'S BUSINESS CHIEFS REALLY HAVE BEEN HAND IN GLOVE WITH THE MAFIA?

films ant TV programmes devoted to it. The murder of radical black American leader Malcolm X, and even the death of film star Marilyn Monroe, have also attracted their fair share of speculation, and we'll also discuss these cases.

Many conspiracy theories relate to the existence of Secret Societies, and we'll be looking into several of these. We'll investigate The Bilderberg Group and attempt to establish whether this shadowy group is really running out world. And - if you're one of those who noticed that, in the last American Presidential election, both candidates belonged to the same secret society – well, we'll be looking into the weird world of Skull and Bones, the Yale-based organisation whose members include both Presidents Bush. Could it really be the American branch of the Illuminati? And who, or what, is the Illuminati? Formed in 1776, have its members, 'the illuminated ones', really been the secret power behind the throne

throughout modern history?

Religion has always attracted its share of conspiracy theories, too, so we'll take a tour around the strange stories that surround the Holy Grail. Could Mary Magdalen have smuggled Christianity's most precious relic out of the Holy Land and into Western Europe, where it remains hidden to this day? Closer to the present, there is the bizarre death of Roberto Calvi, nicknamed 'God's banker'. Could the Pope's business chiefs really have been hand in glove with the Mafia?

CONSPIRACIES AND THE CULT OF CELEBRITY

The cult of celebrity is one of the hallmarks of the twentieth and twenty-first century, so it is not surprising that, in recent year, many conspiracy theorists have turned their attention away from politics and religion towards the lives and deaths of the famous. We'll look into the allegations that certain celebrities, like

UCTION

Elvis and Tupac Shakur, still remain alive, and ask whether there is any possible evidence to support these notions. And we'll also investigate the even stranger theory that Beatle Paul McCartney is actually dead.

And here we move onto the theories that read like the stuff of science fiction. One of the most enduring conspiracy theories of this type maintains that the moon landings were faked. Could this possibly be true? And what of extraterrestrial happenings and alien visitation? What really happened at Roswell? Or at Rendlesham Forest? Is there life on Mars? And how can we explain crop circles?

STRANGER THAN FICTION

Conspiracy theories, then, come in all shapes and sizes. There are those that seem to be taken from the pages of science fiction novels or thrillers. Indeed, many of them do crop up in popular fiction, not least Dan Brown's enormously popular *Da Vinci Code*, which draws off a whole tradition of Holy Grail conspiracies dating back for over thousand years. Yet while many conspiracy theories are more entertaining than realistic, there are some that reveal genuinely disturbing information and ask important questions about secrecy in the way we are governed and receive information.

In the end it is for you, the reader, to decide which theories to believe, and which to dismiss. So turn the page, and prepare to enter into a world much stranger than fiction: the world of the conspiracy theory.

JUST BECAUSE THEY SAY YOU ARE PARANOID, DOESN'T MEAN THEY AREN'T WATCHING YOU.

CHAPTER ONE:

In the wake of the US government's declaration of a 'war on terror' in 2001 came the questions and the theories. What happened on 11 September 2001 as terrorists crashed hijacked airliners into the World Trade Center and the Pentagon?

DID THE US GOVERNMENT ACTUALLY *CARRY OUT* THE

9/11: What really happened on September 11, 2001?

Conspiracy theorists point to the unwillingness of the United States Government to hold a full inquiry into the events of September 11, 2001. Dick Cheney initially opposed an investigation into the terrorist attacks. His reason was that resources and personnel would be taken away from the war on terrorism. It was over a year before the official investigation finally began. By contrast, the investigations into the attack on Pearl Harbor and the assassination of President Kennedy began after only nine and seven days respectively. When the 9/11 investigation finally got under way a number of inconsistent explanations were offered in response to questions relating to matters such as the failure of the military to prevent the attacks.

Perhaps the key to the prevalence of conspiracy theories is not so much the physical evidence as the belief that because of an ulterior motive the government condoned, or even positively encouraged, the terrible attacks. In the most popular of those theories, which was given a boost by the Michael Moore film *Fahrenheit 9/11*, it is reasoned that the United States Government, dominated by powerful neo-conservatives and the oil business, welcomed the disaster in order to rally public support for a war in the Middle East. Although such a war would purport to be a war on terror it would

really be a war for oil. It would also have the effect of increasing defence spending, which would be good for the government-linked defence industry. Finally it would also allow the passage of repressive new legislation, such as the USA Patriot Act which granted extra powers to the Federal Government. Seen from this conspiratorial point of view, the events of September 11 were basically a present-day re-staging of the attack on Pearl Harbor or the sinking of the *Lusitania*, during which catastrophes (at least if you believe the conspiracy version) a government stood by and watched its own people massacred in order that it could drum up support for an unpopular war.

This is a scenario that has persuaded many, particularly in the wake of the widely unpopular war in Iraq. But is it really credible? Does any of it really add up to proof that the United States Government stood by and watched its citizens die?

Not according to *Popular Mechanics* magazine. This publication assembled a panel of experts and went through the theories relating to the destruction of the WTC twin towers. The findings of its experts suggested that some aspects of the collapse of the towers were unusual

RIGHT: Smoke billows from the North Tower of the World Trade Center shortly after American Airlines flight 11 crashed into it at 8.46 am local time.

ABOVE: CAUGHT ON CAMERA: THE DRAMATIC
SCENES AS FLIGHT 175 IS FLOWN BY THE
HIJACKERS DIRECTLY INTO THE SOUTH TOWER OF
THE WORLD TRADE CENTER, SOME 20 MINUTES
AFTER THE ATTACK ON THE NORTH TOWER.

but not impossible – and, after all, how many times in the past have similar events taken place, thereby providing a comparison? In addition, the remainder of the "evidence" – the alleged cancellation of flights by Pentagon officials on the day of the attacks, for instance – was just as likely to be made up of a series of simple coincidences as anything more sinister. Also, the President's odd behaviour on hearing the news may simply have been a kind of panicked paralysis.

Overall, the suggestion that the government actively allowed the 9/11 attacks to take place is extremely far-fetched. The charge of incompetence is rather more likely to stick, of course, although the fact that enormous amounts of intelligence reach the United States Government every day should be borne in mind.

On the other hand, it is hard to dismiss the allegation that the United States Government and the oil and defence

RIGHT: THE NORTH TOWER BEGINS ITS
SPECTACULAR COLLAPSE, ACCOMPANIED BY THE
MUSHROOM CLOUD OF CONCRETE DUST. THIS
CLOUD HAS LED MANY TO CONCLUDE THAT
EXPLOSIVES WERE USED TO COLLAPSE THE TOWER.

industries have done very well out of the War on Terror that followed the events of September 11. This was one cloud whose lining had rather a lot of silver in it, especially if you were a Haliburton shareholder. As a result, the United States Government may well be open to accusations that it has used the 9/11 tragedy to help its friends make profits – but that is quite a different thing from suborning mass murder. The conspiracy theorists may ultimately have a point, but to claim that the United States Government masterminded the attacks is, in most people's view, stretching credibility more than a little far.

THE WTC TWIN TOWERS DEBATE

The events of September 11 have produced what must be the most widely viewed news footage ever shot. On the face of it, you might think that there is no mystery at all about the events that have been so famously recorded. Arab terrorists hijacked four aircraft before flying two of them into the World Trade Center, another into the Pentagon and the fourth into a Pennsylvania field. Al-Qaeda claimed responsibility. Given that Al-Qaeda is not only a terrorist organization with a deep hatred of the United States but is also responsible for a previous attack on the World Trade Center, that is the end of the story, surely?

Well, not as far as the conspiracy theorists are concerned. They maintain that what we saw was a staged political stunt. And who was responsible? Why, the

United States Government of course. Depending on which version of the theory you subscribe to, the government either allowed a real Al-Qaeda attack to take place without preventing it or they carried out the whole operation themselves. So what possible evidence could there be for such an apparently outrageous supposition?

CONSPIRACY THEORISTS MAINTAIN THAT 9/11 WAS A STAGED POLITICAL STUNT

Much of the more responsible conspiracy speculation focuses upon the lead-up to the attacks. As detailed in the section of this book that deals with the Bush–Bin Laden connection (p. 28), the United States Government was supplied with a considerable amount of intelligence that suggested that Al-Qaeda were planning an attack. While most of us might be inclined to put the government's lack of reaction down to incompetence, the more cynically minded see it as part of a deliberate pattern.

Let us begin by looking at the key events in detail, starting with the incident in which the two aircraft crashed into the twin towers of the WTC. To most observers, what happened seems simple enough: planes hit towers and explode, towers fall down. But it wasn't long before this version of the events became the subject of apparently well-informed speculation. The debate focused on whether or not the impact of the aircraft, coupled with the subsequent fire, would really be enough to bring down such huge structures.

What really brought down the twin towers?

According to some experts, buildings 1, 2, and 7 of the World Trade Center are the only steel frame structures in history to have collapsed because of fire. Particularly controversial, because it had not been hit by an aircraft at all, is the fate of building number 7 of the World Trade Center, which collapsed some hours after the two main towers. Furthermore, according to one demolition expert, the huge clouds of concrete dust that were seen billowing out of the towers were symptomatic of an explosion rather than a fire. Other alleged experts claim that the way in which the towers fell straight down had every appearance of controlled demolition. Finally, the wreckage from the towers appeared to contain molten steel. Fire would not cause steel to become molten – but a bomb would. The conspiracy theorists are clear about what these

alleged facts add up to. They claim that the towers of the World Trade Center must have been rigged with explosives in order to make sure that the disaster was as dramatic as possible. Then there is the Pentagon. The plane that crashed into the Pentagon was able to fly towards the building for forty minutes without being intercepted, despite the existence of sophisticated radar technology and anti-missile batteries – not to mention the building's proximity to Andrews Air Force Base. When the aircraft finally hit the building it collided with the west wing, which was nearly empty at the time because of construction work. Once again, government complicity is the clear implication of this event to the conspiracy theorists. Perhaps the most famous piece in this particular conspiracy jigsaw is the notorious footage of President Bush reading a story to children in a kindergarten at the time that an aide announced that the first plane had struck the WTC. Instead of leaping into action the President simply carried on reading the story. In Michael Moore's film *Fahrenheit 9/11* the footage was used to provide the implication that Bush knew exactly what was going on. Further suspicious behaviour, in the eyes of the conspiracy theorists, came in the days following the attack. The government has neither produced the voice recorders nor the flight data recorders ("black boxes") from the aircraft that were involved in the New York attack. That has never happened in any previous major domestic crash. They have

also failed to comment on whether or not the black boxes were recovered from the wreckage. There are also anomalies relating to the identity of the hijackers. Given the general level of decimation, much doubt has been cast on the discovery, near the twin towers, of an undamaged passport belonging to one of the hijackers. Furthermore, the identities of the nineteen hijackers are much disputed. Waleed al-Shehri, one of the men named as being a hijacker by the FBI on their 9/11 attacks web page, has turned up alive and protested his innocence. The identities of three other hijackers are also now in doubt.

FLIGHT 93: THE TRUE STORY

The story of Flight 93, the fourth of the planes to be hijacked on September 11, has become a modern legend. The passengers on Flight 93 were in a different

LEFT: THE PENTAGON WHERE IT WAS STRUCK BY AN AIRLINER ON 9/11. CRTICS OF THE OFFICIAL EXPLANATION CLAIM THAT THE ORIGINAL HOLE WAS TOO SMALL TO HAVE BEEN MADE BY A 757.

situation to those in the other aircraft, who cannot have known that the hijackers were planning to turn the planes into flying bombs. On Flight 93, however, thanks to the mobile phone, passengers were soon made all too aware of what was planned for them. Their plane was in the Washington region so it was more than likely that they were heading for the White House. If they just sat there and did nothing they were certain to die. Gradually, as we know from the final anguished phone calls to loved ones, the passengers decided to fight back. One of them, Todd Beamer, uttered the immortal words: "Let's roll".

in order that many more would be saved. They have been given the status of American heroes.

Today, there are not many who would dispute that the passengers were indeed heroes. However, there are plenty who wonder just exactly what caused the plane to plummet to the earth in such a way and who question the received story of the events.

The final phone call

Essentially, the crash of Flight 93 is the subject of two alternative theories. The first of these maintains that there was an explosion on board the plane. This notion is given substance by the fact that in his final phone call a passenger said that one of the hijackers claimed to be carrying a

AS PASSENGERS ON FLIGHT 93 BEGAN TO FIGHT BACK, TODD BEAMER UTTERED THE NOW FAMOUS WORDS, "LET'S ROLL".

And then there was silence. No more phone calls. The next thing anyone knows for certain is that Flight 93, a Boeing 757, crashed in rural Pennsylvania, near the town of Shanksville. The accepted story is that the passengers rose up and wrested control from the hijackers and that in the course of the struggle the plane went out of control and plunged into the ground. The passengers had sacrificed their lives

bomb. The remaining option is that the aircraft was shot down on the orders of the United States Government before it could hit its target. This is the theory that has aroused much controversy with its suggestion that the government could have authorized the deaths of its own people.

So what evidence is there to suggest that such a thing might have happened?

Well, first there is the timescale. By the time Flight 93 crashed everyone knew what had happened to the WTC twin towers and the Pentagon. A frantic search of United States airspace was taking place in order to establish whether or not any other planes had been hijacked. The United States Government acknowledges that the first fighters with the mission to intercept took off at 8.52 a.m. and another set of fighters took off from Andrews Air Force Base near Washington at 9.35 a.m. – precisely the time that Flight 93 turned through almost 180 degrees and started heading straight for Washington. At that time the F-16s were no more than ten minutes flying time away, yet it was to be another thirty minutes before Flight 93 crashed. Surely one would have expected one of the F-16s to have reached the plane well before 10.06 a.m.?

To back up this line of thinking, there is evidence from a federal flight controller, published a few days later in New Hampshire. He said that an F-16 had been "in hot pursuit" of the hijacked United jet and "must have seen the whole thing". Also, immediately before the crash took place CBS television briefly reported that two F-16 fighters were tailing Flight 93. All

fairly suspicious, but the question remains: would the United States Government shoot its own plane down like that?

On 16 September Vice-President Dick Cheney announced that President Bush had authorized the Air Force pilots to shoot down hijacked commercial aircraft. This statement strongly supports the allegation that the F-16s that took off from Washington had been ordered to "protect the White House at all costs".

SURELY ONE WOULD HAVE EXPECTED ONE OF THE SCRAMBLED F-16S TO HAVE REACHED THE PLANE WELL BEFORE 10.06 A.M.?

ABOVE: WORKERS AND INVESTIGATERS CONTINUE
TO SEARCH THE CRASH SITE OF UNITED FLIGHT 93
IN RURAL PENNSYLVANIA NEAR SHANKSVILLE.

One might expect that the crash scene would offer a clear indication as to whether the aircraft was hit by a missile in the air or had simply hit the ground. This is where the controversy really starts to rage. Conspiracy theorists are convinced that the forensic evidence points to the plane having been brought down by a mid-air impact. The key evidence they cite is the wide dispersal of the aircraft's debris. Letters and other light refuse from the plane were discovered eight miles from the scene of the crash. The aircraft had disintegrated into pieces no more than two inches long and a section of one of the engines, which in itself weighed a ton,

was found 600 yards from the site of the crash. Other remains of the plane were found two miles away near a town called Indian Lake. Furthermore, the debris was not scattered evenly along the route between the different sites but was grouped into distinct clusters. This, the conspiracy theorists argue, is clear evidence that debris was blown out of the plane by an initial midair explosion.

The mysterious white plane
The FBI, for its part, waved these suspicions away. The paper debris that was found eight miles away, they said, was blown there by the wind, while the engine section flew 600 yards due to the force of the aircraft's impact with the ground. They concluded that: "Nothing

was found that was inconsistent with the plane going into the ground intact."

And if all this was not enough there is one final mystery that the conspiracy theorists point to: the mystery of the "white plane". Several eyewitnesses reported seeing a white plane flying very low just before Flight 93 crashed. At first the FBI denied that there had been any such plane in the neighbourhood. Then, as eyewitnesses continued to insist that they had seen such an aircraft, they announced that there had been a plane after all, a civilian business jet. Because it had been flying within twenty miles of Flight 93 the authorities had requested the pilot to

LEFT: DEENA BURNETT, WIDOW OF UNITED FLIGHT 93 VICTIM THOMAS BURNETT JR., LOOKS AT A MEMORIAL PLAQUE SET UP IN FRONT OF THE SPOT WHERE UNITED FLIGHT 93 CRASHED IN SHANKSVILLE.

orders to land at the nearest airport. Secondly, at a time of such uncertainty, and with F-16s supposedly in the vicinity, it seems utterly implausible that the military would seek assistance from the pilot of a civilian aircraft that just happened to be in the area.

So do the conspiracy theorists have a case? The evidence that F-16s *did* catch up with Flight 93 is certainly troubling, as is the pattern of the debris from the crash. And it is hard to believe that the government would have simply allowed the plane to come any closer to Washington. On the other hand, none of the witnesses to the aircraft's eventual crash reported it as having being consumed by a fireball. So if it was hit by a missile it certainly did not explode on impact. Perhaps consideration should be given to the less discussed possibility that one of the terrorists on board may have been carrying a bomb. It certainly ties all the elements of the story together: the heroic passengers take on the hijackers, then one of the hijackers accidentally or deliberately detonates the bomb, and the aircraft plunges to the ground before the pursuing F-16s are forced to confront the option of killing a plane-load of their fellow citizens. Whatever the full truth of the matter, what remains undeniable is the courage of the passengers who were caught up in this terrible situation.

descend from 37,000ft to 5,000ft in order to survey the crash site and transmit the map co-ordinates "for responding emergency crews". If anything, this explanation made the conspiracy theorists all the more suspicious. Firstly, by this time all non-military aircraft within the United States airspace had received clear

THE BUSH–BIN LADEN CONNECTION: JUST HOW CLOSE ARE THESE TWO FAMILIES?

ABOVE: GEORGE W. BUSH WITH MEMBERS OF THE SAUDI ROYAL FAMILY AT HIS RANCH IN TEXAS. US-SAUDI RELATIONS ARE CORDIAL, BUT IS BUSH OVER-FRIENDLY WITH THE WRONG INDIVIDUALS IN THE KINGDOM?

To put it mildly, some conspiracy theories seem far-fetched, depending as they do on the most unlikely details. However, the events upon which some theories are based are so outlandish that speculation is difficult to avoid. The theories that link the Bush and Bin Laden families started with just such an event. Consider this: on the morning of September 11, when a group of terrorists masterminded by Osama Bin Laden were bringing terror to an America led by President George W. Bush, the President's father, George Bush Snr., was in a business meeting at the Ritz Carlton Hotel in Washington with one of Osama Bin Laden's brothers.

So, coincidence or conspiracy? Well, as coincidences go it is a pretty extraordinary one. Yes, the Bush and the Bin Laden families are both involved in the oil business, but is their relationship purely commercial with no link to the events of 9/11? Unsurprisingly, there are plenty of people who believe that the Bushes and the Bin Ladens are politically, as well as financially, linked. Among them is the film-maker Michael Moore, whose film *Fahrenheit 9/11* made much of the links between the two families. Craig Unger did the same with his best-selling book, *House of Bush, House of Saud*.

So let us examine the case for conspiracy, starting with a history of the links between the Bushes and the Bin Ladens. The connection begins in Houston, Texas, during the seventies, when George W. Bush was just starting out in his family's two businesses of

politics and oil. The Bin Laden family helped fund his first venture into oil. The connection came through a man named Jim Bath, a friend of George W. Bush since his days with the Texas Air National Guard, the position that kept him out of the Vietnam War.

THE SAUDI INVESTORS

By the late seventies Bath was an entrepreneur with links to the CIA, an organization headed by George Bush Senr. from 1976 onwards. At around that time, Bath entered into a trust agreement with Salem Bin Laden, older brother of Osama, whereby Bath would act as the Bin Laden family's representative in North America, investing money in various business ventures. In turn this led to Bath becoming the business representative of Khalid bin Mahfouz, a member of the family who owned the National Commercial Bank, the principal bank of the Saudi royal family.

In 1978 Bath took on a partner, a former navy pilot called Charles W. White, who would run his real estate company. Both the Bin Laden and the bin Mahfouz families invested in this company and on their behalf Bath bought an airport, as well as office and apartment buildings. Later on, he purchased a mansion in River Oaks, Houston. That same year, George W. Bush started up an oil company called Arbusto 78. Thanks to his connection with Bath, initial investors in this new company included Salem Bin Laden and Khalid bin Mahfouz.

Despite the Saudi investment (at least $1 million according to White), Bush's ventures into the oil industry were not a success and by 1987 his various oil companies had been taken over by another company, Harken Energy. That year Harken had a $25-million stock offering underwritten by financiers connected to the soon-to-be-infamous BCCI (Bank of Credit and Commerce International), a Middle Eastern banking concern.

Over the next few years the BCCI was exposed as a massively corrupt criminal enterprise which had been stealing from its own investors in addition to being involved in money laundering and the Iran contra scandal. The bank also helped finance a whole range of the most unsavoury figures of recent history including Saddam Hussein, Manuel Noriega and terrorist leader Abu Nidal. One of the men who were caught up in the scandal was none other than bin Mahfouz, who was discovered to have withdrawn substantial investments from the bank just before its assets were seized. The charges against him were only dropped when he made a huge payment of $225 million into a Federal Reserve settlement account followed by one of $245 million to BCCI's court-appointed liquidators.

The first Gulf War, led by US President George Bush Snr., took place while the BCCI scandal was rumbling on. Many saw this as a war for oil, in which a president with a background in the oil business made sure that Iraq did not gain a stranglehold on world oil markets.

THE FUNDAMENTALIST

Meanwhile, Osama Bin Laden had emerged as an important figure in Saudi Arabia. While his family had concentrated on their business interests, he had become a firebrand who had led Islamic fighters in the CIA-backed campaign against the Russians in Afghanistan. However, while his brothers were happy to maintain commercial links with the United States, Osama believed that the Islamic states should control their own destinies. He therefore urged the Saudis to fight Saddam Hussein themselves rather than leave the job to the Americans. When the United States left 20,000 troops behind in Saudi Arabia after the war, Bin Laden was enraged. Soon afterwards, he left Saudi Arabia for Sudan, where he built up a terrorist organization which shortly became known as Al-Qaeda. The group was dedicated to eradicating the United States presence in the Islamic Holy Lands.

Over the next decade Al-Qaeda launched a whole series of operations against the United States. In 1993 the organization made a spectacular attempt to blow up the World Trade Center, which caused considerable loss of life and only narrowly failed to destroy the entire building. In 1995 five American soldiers were killed in a car bomb in Saudi Arabia.

In 1996 the Sudanese Government decided that they did not want Osama to remain in their country and so they asked him to leave, together with his organization. At this time, the United States had the opportunity to arrest him but made no effort to do so. In 1998, Al-Qaeda blew up the United States embassies in Kenya and Tanzania, resulting in the deaths of 224 people.

In January 2000, intelligence sources discovered that a meeting of Al-Qaeda leaders was taking place in Kuala Lumpur in Malaysia. Attending the meeting was Khalid Shaykh Mohammed, the number three man in Al-Qaeda and the mastermind behind the 1998 attacks on United States embassies. (He is also presumed to be the man responsible for the attack on the USS *Cole* and, above all, the 9/11 attacks.) Also present at the meeting were Khalid al-Mihdhar and Nawaf al-Hazmi, two Saudi citizens who ended up as hijackers on Flight 77, the plane that crashed into the Pentagon on September 11.

BELOW: OSAMA BIN LADEN, WITH CHIEF LIEUTENANT, THE EGYPTIAN AYMAN AL-ZAWAHIRI, A MAN MANY THINK IS THE REAL BRAIN BEHIND THE AL-QAEDA NETWORK.

Warning signs ignored

The CIA knew of the meeting and asked the Malaysian secret police to place it under surveillance. Video footage was taken, as well as photographs of the dozen men in attendance. Nevertheless, al-Hazmi and al-Mihdhar flew to the United States on their own passports after the meeting broke up, landing in Los Angeles. There they were met by Omar al-Bayoumi, a Saudi national who worked for the Saudi civil aviation authority. Al-Bayoumi took al-Mihdhar and al-Hazmi to San Diego, where he put them up in an apartment, enrolled them in flight school and gave them money. Later, the FBI concluded that it was most likely that al-Bayoumi was a Saudi intelligence agent. Al-Bayoumi also passed on thousands of dollars to the hijackers. The money came from Princess Haifa, wife of Prince Bandar Saudi, ambassador to the United States.

That September, al-Hazmi and al-Mihdhar moved into the home of a local imam in San Diego, Abdussattar Shaikh. The imam was an FBI informant who held meetings with his FBI handler while al-Hazmi and al-Mihdhar sat in a room next door. Shaikh would later claim that he was never told what mission the hijackers were on. His FBI handler, meanwhile, was never informed by his superiors to look out for al-Hazmi and al-Mihdhar.

During the following months, Al-Qaeda launched an attack, killing seventeen sailors, on the USS *Cole*, which was sitting in a harbour off the coast of Yemen. Throughout 2001, in the months leading

During the following months, Al-Qaeda launched an attack on the USS Cole, killing 17

up to September 11, the CIA, FBI and National Security Agency received intelligence that a terrorist attack of some magnitude was going to be launched by Al-Qaeda. However, in May of that year Khalid Shaykh Mohammed, architect of the 9/11 atrocities and Al-Qaeda's other attacks, was able to travel freely into the United States. Then, in August 2001, President Bush received a detailed and lengthy daily briefing from the CIA in which Al-Qaeda's aim of launching an attack against the United States was mentioned, together with the name of Osama Bin Laden. To this day, the Bush White House refuses to release the contents of this briefing to Congressional inquiries into the events of 9/11. Did loyalty to his old Saudi friends cloud Bush's judgment? If so, he paid a terrible price, because in the following month, on September 11, 2001, the long-feared attack was finally made.

And that, of course, is where we came

in, with the fact that on the morning of the attack George Bush Snr. was at a meeting of members of the Carlyle Group in Washington, along with Bin Laden's own brother. To compound the irony – if irony it was – members of the Bin Laden family were allowed to leave the United States without questioning two days later.

There are two possible explanations. One is that the Bush family and the Bin Laden family are essentially businessmen with oil interests. The fact that various Bushes may have become presidents of the United States or that one of the huge Bin Laden clan should have become a terrorist leader is essentially irrelevant. The Bushes therefore understood that the Bin Laden family in general could not be held responsible for the actions of the black sheep Osama, and simply helped them leave the country before they could become the victims of ill-informed speculation.

On the other hand, there are the conspiracy theories. Perhaps the most compelling of these is the suggestion that the closeness of the connection between the Bush family and Saudi oil interests actually influenced the President's attitude to Saudi Arabia. The followers of these theories suspect that because of the involvement of Saudi Arabia the evidence pointing to a pending attack was not followed up as thoroughly as it might have been. The importance of Saudi oil – not just to the Bush family, but to wider American interests – has meant that the country has not been asked hard questions about human rights or about its support for Islamic terrorism. The simpler fact is that fifteen of the nineteen 9/11 hijackers were Saudi citizens. So why was Saudi Arabia not the focus of American anger? Why was all the military attention turned first on Afghanistan and then on the aggressively secular and one-time American ally Iraq?

These are, of course, difficult questions to answer and perhaps this is an area where the conspiracy theories overlap with more conventional politics. George W. Bush may well have turned a blind eye to the activities of his family friends the Bin Ladens. Perhaps more importantly, however, the oil interests between the two countries meant that American political leaders in general failed to bring Saudi Arabia to account for its terrorist activities – with devastating results, as it would eventually turn out.

GEORGE W. BUSH MAY WELL HAVE TURNED A BLIND EYE TO THE ACTIVITIES OF HIS FAMILY FRIENDS THE BIN LADENS.

The Afghan Pipeline

Many popular conspiracy theories of modern times centre around one particular product: black gold, or oil as it is more generally known. In particular these theories suggest that United States foreign policy in the wake of September 11 has not been driven by the desire to wage war on terror but by the desire to gain control of more and more of the world's oil supply.

In the case of the war in Iraq, it is easy to see why such a theory has arisen. After all, Iraq is a major oil producer and the United States is undeniably hungry for oil. But in the case of Afghanistan the charge seems rather more far-fetched. Afghanistan doesn't actually have any oil. So why was it that within days of the decision by the United States to invade Afghanistan conspiracy theorists were starting to suggest that the invasion was really all about oil?

"It's all about oil"

The answer to that is simple. According to the conspiracy theorists, the United States wanted to gain control of Afghanistan in order to build a pipeline through the country. Oil could then be brought from the landlocked Caspian Sea in the former Soviet Union to the Indian Ocean. Apparently, a firm called Unocal had made plans for just such a pipeline but had ditched them when the Taliban came to power. Afghanistan was then considered to be too dangerous to risk such a large investment.

The real reason for the American invasion then, according to the conspiracy theorists, was not to root out Osama Bin Laden and his Al-Qaeda terrorists but to overthrow an anti-American regime and make it safe to build an American oil pipeline through the country, a cause dear to George W. Bush's heart, being an oilman himself. This is the story that spread over the internet and into legitimate newspapers across Europe. The mantra of anti-war protestors became "it's all about oil". But does the theory stand up?

The short answer is – not really. First of all, one of the things the conspiracy theorists managed to overlook was that the Unocal pipeline project was for gas not oil. Secondly if Unocal and/or the United States Government really only cared about getting their pipeline built, they would have been better off coming to an agreement with the Taliban, who did at least control most of Afghanistan. Instead, the war has made the country less safe, rather than safer, for business.

Conspiracy theorists point out, however, that the new government of Afghanistan has got together with the gas- and oil-rich Central Asian republic of Turkmenistan and has now agreed in principle to build a pipeline. The key words here, though, are "in principle".The government of Afghanistan may well be keen on the idea of having a lucrative pipeline running through the country, but

there is absolutely no sign that any major western oil company wants anything to do with it. The fact is that the oil and gas companies have looked around for another option for their pipelines. Afghanistan may provide the shortest route to the ocean but it is not the only one. A new pipeline that runs in a very different direction was quietly built, therefore: it was completed in 2005.

The "Rose Revolution"

The pipeline in question is 1,090 miles long and it runs from the town of Baku in the oil-rich country of Azerbaijan through Georgia and on to the seaport of Ceyhan in Turkey. It is a project that has had a profound impact on the politics of the Caucasus region but it has mostly been ignored by the world's media, who have focused instead on the more sensational Afghan pipeline story.

In fact, if there is a conspiracy going on it is a rather more subtle one than has previously been suggested. While fingers have been pointed at the United States over Afghanistan, she has been quietly playing a large part in the introduction of a more US-friendly regime to the former Soviet country of Georgia, through which the new pipeline passes.

ABOVE: MEMBERS OF THE TALIBAN TAKE A BREAK FROM ENFORCING RELIGIOUS PURITY, AFGHANISTAN. ALTHOUGH INITIALLY SUPPORTED BY THE US, THE TALIBAN WOULD QUICKLY BECOME A LEADING MEMBER OF THE 'AXIS OF EVIL'.

The United States has spent vast amounts in support of the so-called "Rose Revolution" in Georgia, which ushered the American-educated Mikhail Saakashvili into power. America's new ties with Georgia were clearly demonstrated when George Bush became the first United States president to visit the country. And as for the Turkish port where the pipeline ends, it is no surprise to discover that it is right next to the American airbase at Incirlik.

So there is plenty of evidence to suggest that oil and gas interests play a major part in the foreign policy decisions of the United States. And there is also no question that the huge reserves of gas and oil in Central Asia are a major prize. However, the conspiracy theorists seem to have missed a trick for once when it comes to Georgia. And as for the Afghan war? Well, it might just be the case that America did after all invade the country to attempt to rid the world of the terrorists who had so recently struck at its heart, rather than to build a pipeline that they could easily build somewhere else.

THE OKLAHOMA CITY BOMBING

At the time that it was carried out – 19 April 1995 – the Oklahoma City bombing was the worst terrorist atrocity ever perpetrated on American soil. That grim record was comprehensively trumped six years later by the events of September 11, but at the time the Oklahoma bombing was a huge shock to the American system. What made it especially traumatic was the fact that it was not carried out by foreigners – Russians, Iraqis or any other perceived enemies of America – but by Americans. Many Americans found this difficult to believe, which is perhaps why

LEFT: THE ALFRED P. MURRAGH FEDERAL BUILDING, OKLAHOMA CITY AFTER IT WAS BOMBED BY EX-SOLDIER WITH A GRUDGE TIMOTHY MCVEIGH ON 19 APRIL, 1995. THE ATTACK WAS THE WORST TERRORIST OUTRAGE ON US SOIL UNTIL 9/11.

conspiracy theories very quickly grew up around the event. The suggestion was that it was the work of outsiders. Some of these theories can be dismissed, but there remain doubts about just exactly who was responsible for the bombing. Did Timothy McVeigh and his friends act entirely independently, as was argued at McVeigh's trial? Or was McVeigh simply a cog in a much bigger conspiracy that involved a whole gang of far-right activists?

The essential facts are not in question. In the early morning of 19 April 1995, Timothy McVeigh drove a rented yellow truck up to the Alfred P. Murrah federal building in Oklahoma City. He parked the truck in a parking space for the handicapped, just beneath an infant day-care centre. The truck was loaded with a huge and lethal fertilizer bomb, consisting of more than 6,000lbs of ammonium nitrate soaked in nitromethane fuel, plus an additional quantity of commercial Tovex explosive. The whole lot was wired up to blasting caps. At around 8.53 a.m., after

he had parked the truck, McVeigh lit two fuses and walked quickly away, heading for his getaway car. He was wearing a T-shirt emblazoned with "Sic semper tyrannis", the words that were shouted by John Wilkes Booth as he assassinated Abraham Lincoln.

Before McVeigh could reach the vehicle he was knocked off his feet by the force of the explosion he had set off. Windows were smashed and buildings shook around him as he headed towards his getaway car, an 18-year-old Mercury Marquis. McVeigh got into the car and might well have made good his escape if it had not been for the fact that he was pulled over by a highway patrolman for not having a rear licence plate. When the patrolman checked the car he found that McVeigh had a concealed firearm. The patrolman proceeded to take him into custody, little suspecting at this point that he had caught the man responsible for a bomb that had killed 168 people, injured 800 more, traumatized an entire city and shaken a nation.

WAS THERE A SECOND MAN?
Within forty-eight hours, though, the investigating officers had figured out that

MCVEIGH WAS WEARING A T-SHIRT EMBLAZONED WITH "SIC SEMPER TYRANNIS", THE SAME WORDS SHOUTED BY JOHN WILKES BOOTH.

LEFT: TIMOTHY MCVEIGH IN COURT. MCVEIGH MANAGED TO EVADE THE FORCES OF JUSTICE AFTER THE OKLAHOMA BOMBING FOR AROUND THREE HOURS BEFORE BEING ARRESTED FOR DRIVING A CAR WITH NO LICENCE PLATE, POSSIBLY NOT AN INDICATION OF A CRIMINAL MASTERMIND.

the guy with the missing licence plate was indeed the bomber they were looking for. At the time, however, that did not appear to be the end of the matter. The FBI were known to be looking for a second man, whom they believed to have been directly involved in the bombings. Gradually, though, this line of investigation seemed to peter out and when the case came to trial it was McVeigh alone who was

MCVEIGH ALONE WAS ACCUSED OF PLANTING THE BOMB, DULY CONVICTED OF MURDER AND SENTENCED TO DEATH.

accused of actually planting the bomb. He was duly convicted of murder and was sentenced to death, being executed by lethal injection at a US penitentiary in Terre Haute, Indiana, on 11 June 2001.

However, the question the conspiracy theorists wanted an answer to was – did McVeigh act alone or not? There is plenty of evidence to suggest that he did not. In the early stages of the investigation, the FBI were convinced that he had at least one partner in the operation. Numerous witnesses who saw McVeigh on the day of the bombing claim to have seen him with another man. They also claim to have seen a brown pick-up truck following the yellow Ryder truck. By some accounts, McVeigh and the second man were seen leaving the Murrah Building in the pick-up truck at just after 8 a.m., before returning in the yellow Ryder truck. At 8.45 a.m. the Ryder truck stopped at a convenience store and McVeigh was seen to buy two cokes and a packet of cigarettes, even though he was a non-smoker. Another eyewitness claimed to have seen McVeigh get into the Mercury along with another man. In all, at least ten different eyewitness statements suggested that there was at least one other person with McVeigh on the morning of the bombing.

All of that explains why the FBI spent the next year looking for a mystery second man, but it does not explain why, after a year's fruitless searching, they decided instead to promote the lone bomber theory in court. The idea that McVeigh did not act alone was awarded further credence when he was put through a polygraph test by his defence team. He passed on all questions concerning his own role but he failed when he denied that anybody else was involved.

It may well be that the FBI did not change their approach because of any sinister conspiracy but for the simple reason that they had a case against

McVeigh and they were worried that the trial might collapse if the existence of an unknown second man was brought into the equation. It would have been easy for McVeigh to attempt to shift the responsibility onto this unknown man. If that was the case, the tactic was successful: McVeigh was found guilty. However, it did lead to unusual anomalies during the trial, such as the FBI's refusal to call any witnesses to McVeigh's movements (because they would all have

bombing, but had then become a key FBI informant, was sentenced to twelve years in prison on 27 May 1998 on the charge of failing to warn the authorities about the attack.

The role played by Terry Nichols was harder to assess. At his federal trial, alongside McVeigh, he was sentenced to life imprisonment. In 2004 he was tried again, this time on state murder charges in Oklahoma, and was convicted of 160 counts of first-degree murder. The jury,

NO ONE IDENTIFIED THE MYSTERY MAN AND THE STORY THAT McVEIGH WAS A LONE BOMBER BECAME THE ACCEPTED TRUTH.

mentioned that there was another man with him). Privately, the FBI appear to have suspected that the second man died in the blast. There was one gruesome piece of evidence remaining after the bombing – a left leg whose owner had never been identified. Might the leg have belonged to the second man?

Whatever the case, no one identified the mystery man and the story that McVeigh was a lone bomber became the generally accepted truth.

Two of McVeigh's friends, Terry Nichols and Michael Fortier, were subsequently arrested. Both of them had sheltered McVeigh. Michael Fortier, who had sheltered and aided McVeigh before the

however, were deadlocked on the question of whether or not this should result in a death sentence. As a result, the judge sentenced him to life without the possibility of parole.

FAR-RIGHT MILITIAS
That should have been the end of the story. The FBI would certainly have been happy to have drawn a line under this terrible incident. However, it was hardly likely that the conspiracy aficionados would let things rest there. After all, there had been any number of rumours floating around from the very start. Some of the rumours came from those sympathetic to the far right. They were so accustomed to

blaming the Federal Government for everything that they were not prepared to stop now. According to these obsessives, the Oklahoma bombing was actually carried out by the government in order to discredit the far right. There were unfounded allegations that federal employees had been warned not to go into work on the day of the bombing. Similar rumours circulated in the days following the events of September 11.

Rather more plausible is the suggestion that the far right militia movement was actually much more involved in the bombing than the FBI were prepared to admit. Following McVeigh's confession and subsequent conviction, this was the direction in which most conspiracy theorists started to look. In particular some assiduous reporters began to find clear links between McVeigh and a gang of far-right militia men that was connected to the Aryan Republican Army. The gang, led by Peter Langan and Richard Guthrie, carried out a series of bank robberies across the Midwest during the mid-1990s.

Close investigation revealed that McVeigh had been in the same place at the same time as the gang over the years. During those periods he was able to travel continually and he always had money without having a job. He also told friends about a group that he had become involved with. For years, rumours of McVeigh's connection with the gang circulated but for a long time the FBI refused to accept the link. All that changed when, early in 2004, Associated Press revealed that blasting caps of the type used in Oklahoma City had been found at the gang's compound when they were arrested in 1996. Furthermore, the gang were in possession of a driving licence that belonged to a gun dealer who had been robbed by McVeigh immediately before the bombing. These revelations were deeply embarrassing to the FBI and they resulted in an internal inquiry being launched into the matter in March 2004. As yet, however, no conclusions from this inquiry have been made public.

A COVER-UP?

So was there a wider conspiracy or did McVeigh act alone? In this case it definitely looks as if the conspiracy theorists have a point. The evidence of links between McVeigh and the Midwest bank robbers is extremely persuasive, especially when it is backed up by the fact that so many eyewitnesses recalled seeing McVeigh with other men on the day of the bombing. And the reasons for the cover-up? Probably simple incompetence and the desire to make sure that there was a successful outcome at the trial – one that would make a nice neat story and reassure the American people that justice had been done. Unfortunately, the result of this apparent deceit was to further entrench the mistrust of government in the minds of many Americans and make them all the more likely to give credit to outlandish conspiracy theories – like those, indeed, that McVeigh and his cohorts believed in.

CHAPTER TWO:

THROUGHOUT HISTORY, MEN — AND WOMEN, BUT IT IS
PREDOMINANTLY MEN — HAVE FORMED SOCIETIES FOR THE
MUTUAL ADVANCEMENT OF THEIR MEMBERS, TO SHARE ONE
ANOTHER'S PROCLIVITIES, OR SIMPLY TO SOCIALIZE WITH LIKE-

MINDED INDIVIDUALS. THAT SOME OF THESE SOCIETIES HAVE BEEN SECRETIVE, CANNOT BE DENIED. BUT JUST HOW SUSPICIOUS SHOULD WE BE OF THESE MYSTERIOUS GROUPS OF PEOPLE?

THE BILDERBERG GROUP

It may well be the oldest conspiracy theory of all – that the world is controlled by a shadowy cabal of powerful men and women. Often, the existence of such groups is dubious in the extreme – as with, for instance, the Illuminati. In other cases, there may be some basis in fact (for example, it is true that there are many powerful Jewish bankers) but the leap to conspiracy (that Jewish bankers are running the world) is nothing more than the product of a delusion, in this case a form of anti-Semitic paranoia.

However, the Bilderberg Group does at least look as if it might just be the genuine article – a group whose members rule the world. To begin with, it is clear that the

Bilderberg Group does actually exist. It was founded fifty years ago and it has held an annual meeting ever since. And it is undoubtedly a secret organization. It has no corporate presence, not even a website, and it goes to some lengths to keep its annual meeting place – which is different each year – a secret. Finally, it does indeed involve many of the most powerful men, and women, in the world. Henry Kissinger and Paul Wolfowitz are regular attendees as are numerous Rockefellers, Fords and Agnellis. Even more significant, as far as the conspiracy theorists are concerned, is the fact that Margaret Thatcher, Bill Clinton and Tony Blair all attended before they came to lead

their countries. Coincidence? Perhaps. Let us just wait and see whether the Democratic presidential hopeful John Edwards, a Bilderberg guest in 2005, ever makes it to the top job.

Secret meetings

So what are the known facts about this mysterious organization? It was founded in 1954 and it took its name from the hotel in the Netherlands where the first meeting was held. Its founder members were British politician Denis Healey, Joseph Retinger, David Rockefeller and Prince Bernhard of the Netherlands, a man who, it is often pointed out, was a member of the Nazi party in his youth (though how that impacts upon those conspiracy theorists who see the Bilderberg Group as

a Jewish conspiracy is anyone's guess).

The group is still based in the Netherlands, for administrative purposes at least. It maintains an office in the quiet town of Leiden. Phone calls to the office, however, are invariably met with an anonymous answerphone message.

The official purpose of the Bilderberg group, inasmuch as it has been publicly expressed, was to further the understanding between Western Europe and North America through informal meetings between powerful individuals. If it has an agenda, says founder member Lord Healey, it is to promote democracy across the globe. To this end, a steering committee draws up an invitation list each year with up to a hundred names on it, all of them either European or North American. The location of the annual meeting is fixed, with countries taking it in turn to host the meetings. Funding for the conferences is then raised from friendly corporations like Nokia or Fiat, for these conferences are where the top names in politics and industry meet. The list of participants is made available to the public, but the topics of the discussions are not. And attendees have to promise not to reveal what has been said at Bilderberg meetings. This secrecy, of course, has attracted much sceptical coverage and has provided the conspiracy theorists with ammunition.

Bilderbergers themselves claim that it is not secrecy but privacy – and that privacy is essential if prominent people are to be allowed to speak freely, without the fear of media attention.

A DARKER PURPOSE?

One thing is for sure, though. Few people ever turn down an invitation to a Bilderberg event and attending one of their

IS THE BILDERBERG GROUP REALLY A SINISTER CABAL, AS SOME CLAIM?

meetings is almost always a good career move. Some say that this is just the way of the world. There are plenty of exclusive clubs where the rich and powerful meet away from prying eyes: the Bilderberg is simply the most exclusive club of them all.

Its members like to suggest that the Bilderberg Group is a benign organization, a think-tank dedicated to the values of liberal democracy, whose interest is simply in helping the world to run better. Its critics, however, feel that the group has a much darker purpose. They find it hard to believe that an organization that is genuinely committed to democracy should feel the need to shroud its discussions in secrecy. At best, say the critics, the Bilderberg is an engine of globalization, an

organization dedicated to producing a bland new world where we all consume the same goods, watch the same TV shows and believe the same identikit politicians. A world, in short, that is run for profit. Earth plc.

Others feel that the aims of the group are more sinister yet. They claim that the Bilderberg is an actively neo-Nazi organization that is working to build a world fascist state. Others suggest that the Bilderberg Group is simply the latest front organization for the Illuminati, the secret rulers of the world for centuries.

So which of these is the Bilderberg? Benign talking shop or sinister cabal? There seems to be little or no evidence for the more extreme claims. However, the accusation that this is an organization that is committed to globalization seems to have some substance. It is surely no coincidence that one of the delegates in 2005 is Mrs Bill Gates, wife of the supreme globalizer. Yet globalization is hardly a secret matter: one has only to walk down any shopping street from Berlin to Baltimore to see that. Perhaps the truth of the matter is that today, political, media and commercial power is increasingly concentrated in an ever-smaller number of hands, and that the Bilderberg Group is part of that process. It is not so much a shadowy organization of world rulers but an informal group of people whose economic power already dominates our lives, whose brand names are written on almost everything we consume and who wish to further their global interests.

The Illuminati

The Illuminati are one of the great touchstones of conspiracy theory. This is the shadowy group that the conspiracy theorists believe are behind practically everything that takes place in the world – capitalism or communism, Zionism or Catholicism. The British royal family, the American presidency, Freemasons, the Knights Templar, even extra-terrestrials – all of them are bound up with the Illuminati, the secret rulers of the world. And of course the fact that there is no evidence of the existence of the Illuminati is actually proof of their all-powerful nature, rather than of their non-existence.

So who are – or were – the Illuminati and why are they credited with such extraordinary powers? The first part of this question is easy enough to answer. The Illuminati were a group founded in Bavaria, Germany, in the late eighteenth century by an ex-Jesuit named Adam Weishaupt, a professor of canon law in Ingolstadt, Germany. Much taken with the ideas of the Enlightenment, he decided to form a group of fellow republican freethinkers which would be clandestine, because it was dangerous to hold such ideas at that time. Together with one Baron Adolph von Knigge, he founded his movement on 1 May 1776, calling it the "Perfectibilists". However, its adherents soon became known as the Illuminati. They were also sometimes referred to as the Illuminati Order, the Order of the Illuminati or the Bavarian Illuminati.

Many of those attracted to the new movement were already Freemasons, which accounts for the perceived links between the two, quite different, movements. Members had to pledge obedience to their superiors and were divided into three classes. The first class was called the Nursery, and it included the offices of Preparation, Novice, Minerval and Illuminatus Minor; the second was known as the Masonry and it embraced the higher ranks of Illuminatus Major and Illuminatus Dirigens; and the third class was referred to as the Mysteries and

ABOVE: ADAM WEISHAUPT, THE EIGHTEENTH-CENTURY POLITICAL AND RELIGIOUS RADICAL WHO FOUNDED THE SOCIETY KNOWN AS THE ILLUMINATI.

The Order of the Inspirati.   No. 35.

APPOLONI⁹ TYANEUS in Domitians Time.

MAHOMET receives his Law by Inspiration.

ROGER BACON an Inglishman.

EDW.ᵈ KELLY Prophet or Seer to D.ᵈ DEE.

D.ᵈ DEE avoucheth his Stone is brought by Angelical Ministry.

PARACELSUS Receits from the Inspiration of Spirits.

ABOVE: PHILOSOPHER AND SCIENTIST ROGER BACON, THE
TUDOR MYSTIC DR JOHN DEE AND THE MEDIAEVAL
ALCHEMIST PARACELSUS, APPOLONI AND MOHAMMED ARE ALL
CLAIMED AS ILLUMINATI IN THIS SEVENTEENTH-CENTURY
PRINT. THE CLAIM IS SOMEWHAT UNLIKELY, AS LEAST AS FAR
AS MOHAMMED IS CONCERNED.

within it were the Lesser Mysteries, the ranks of Presbyter and Regent and the Greater Mysteries, the highest ranks of Magus and Rex.

The Illuminati managed to start branches in most European countries in the first few years of its existence, with many influential intellectuals and progressive politicians counting themselves as members – among them such luminaries as the great German writer Goethe and the dukes of Gotha and Weimar. The total membership of the group at this point has been estimated at 2,000.

However, the association's radical ideas soon attracted the dislike of the powerful Catholic Church which, in 1784, persuaded the Bavarian Government to pass a law banning all secret societies, including the Illuminati and the Freemasons. According to all the official accounts this resulted in the disappearance of the Illuminati. The order was already suffering from internal schisms and it was finally wound up in 1790.

A SINGLE WORLD GOVERNMENT

No sooner had the Illuminati come to an official end than the conspiracy theories began. Just seven years later, in 1797, a French cleric called Abbé Augustin Barruél published a book called *Memoirs Illustrating the History of Jacobinism*, in which he set out a conspiracy theory involving the Illuminati, along with the Knights Templar, the Rosicrucians and, as

his book title suggests, the Jacobins. In the following year a Scottish professor of natural history named John Robison published the first part of a book with the unwieldy title of *Proofs of a Conspiracy Against all the Religions and Governments of Europe, Carried on in the Secret Meetings of Free Masons, Illuminati, and Reading Societies, Collected from Good Authorities*. Robison's thesis was that an Illuminati conspiracy was planning to replace all religions with humanism and nation states with a single world government.

This linking of the Illuminati with Freemasonry and the further linking of the combined institutions with the sinister manipulation of society began to gain credence. However, not everyone was convinced. No less a person than Thomas Jefferson declared that he could quite understand why the Illuminati had been driven to secrecy:

As Weishaupt lived under the tyranny of a despot and priests, he knew that caution was necessary even in spreading information, and the principles of pure morality... If Weishaupt had written here, where no secrecy is necessary in our endeavours to render men wise and virtuous, he would not have thought of any secret machinery for that purpose.

Of course the conspiracy theorists saw this as proof that Jefferson himself was one of the Illuminati. And, indeed, it was not long before rumours of Illuminati involvement in American affairs began to circulate. The symbol of the all-seeing pyramid in the Great Seal of the United States was cited as being a secret sign, painted by high-ranking members of the Illuminati whose intention was to show how the Illuminati's ever-present watchful eye surveyed the Americans. It has also been suggested that the Yale-based secret society Skull and Bones was founded as the American branch of the Illuminati.

In recent times, conspiracy theories involving the Illuminati have become ever more bizarre. Books and internet sites explain that the Illuminati are responsible for almost everything, whether it be the assassination of President Kennedy or the foundation of the Jehovah's Witnesses. The fact that there is no evidence of the group is always presented as conclusive proof of its secret existence.

EXTRA-TERRESTRIAL REPTILES

Perhaps the most extraordinary of all the Illuminati-linked theories is that put forward by a former British soccer player and sports commentator named David Icke. According to Icke the Illuminati are indeed the secret rulers of the world but they date back a lot further than the Bavaria of the 1780s. In fact, says Icke, the Illuminati are reptilian extra-terrestrials who have controlled the world for thousands of years, and have been operating from the fourth dimension (which explains why we have not noticed them yet).

While Icke's theory has not attracted a huge following, but there are still many who believe that the Illuminati – while not reptilian aliens – do exist. And it may well be true that the world's powerful people do talk discreetly to each other within secret organizations. However, the suggestion that they are linked by membership of the Illuminati, a quasi-Masonic group that is devoted to republican freethinking, seems more than a little unlikely. Or is that just what our reptilian overlords want us to believe...

ABOVE: ONE-TIME GOALKEEPER AND SPORTS PRESENTER DAVID ICKE, NOW A CONSPIRACY THEORIST OF THE FIRST ORDER, AND SCOURGE OF REPTILIAN ALIENS WHEREVER THEY MAY BE HIDING.

Secrets of the Catholic Church

The Knights Templar

The Christian Church has been a natural target for conspiracy theorists throughout almost the whole of its existence. In centuries past, these theorists would have been called heretics and burnt at the stake. In these more enlightened days they post their ideas on the internet and write bestselling novels.

Two subjects that appeal to conspiracy theorists are the Knights Templar and the Holy Grail. The Knights Templar were an order of warrior monks who were based in Jerusalem during the time of the Crusades. They were believed to be fabulously wealthy and they became so powerful that in 1307 Philip IV of France led a campaign against them. Members of the order were arrested and tortured until they confessed to heresy. Their influence lingered on for many years, especially in Portugal and Scotland, but they gradually disappeared from view. However, many theorists believe that the order actually went underground instead of dying out and that it is still in existence.

The Holy Grail

Even more mysterious than the Knights Templar is the Holy Grail, one of the great myths of Christianity. The Holy Grail was supposedly the cup that caught the blood of Jesus during his crucifixion. The story goes that the cup was kept by a friend of Jesus, Joseph of Arimathea, who might have taken it to France, or perhaps even Glastonbury in England. Some believe that it was taken to Jerusalem in the Holy Land: others claim that it has been kept in Genoa, Valencia or Rosslyn Chapel in Scotland. According to some accounts, it might even have fallen into the hands of the Knights Templar. Wherever it landed up, it became a mythical object over time and it was credited with extraordinary magical powers.

Stories have circulated about the Holy Grail and the Knights Templar for centuries, but a modern bestseller Holy Blood, Holy Grail, published in 1982, suggested that behind these mysteries lay an even greater one – one that went to the

BELOW: Members of the military order of the Templars. The order was persecuted for heresy, and then disbanded by the French King Philip IV in 1307, but the conspiracy theories surrounding it have not gone away.

ABOVE: THE RISEN CHRIST APPEARS TO MARY MAGDALENE IN CORREGIO'S PAINTING NOLI ME TANGERE. BUT WAS CHRIST EVER ACTUALLY DEAD?

very heart of the Christian faith. According to the authors of the book, the Holy Grail was not a cup at all: that was the result of a mistake in translation. The real Christian treasure was not the Holy Grail but the Holy Blood. That is, the true secret was not the existence of a mere cup but of a bloodline of the descendants of Jesus.

THE MAGDALENE CONSPIRACY

According to this theory, Jesus had two children, the products of a clandestine marriage to Mary Magdalene. These children, so the story goes, were brought to France by Mary Magdalene and Joseph of Arimathea. The oldest child died but the second son went on to have children whose descendants would become the (real) Merovingian Kings of France between the fifth and eighth centuries AD. After the Merovingian Kings were overthrown, their legacy was protected by the Knights Templar and their great secret – together with the evidence to back it up – was hidden away. Its existence was only hinted at by obscure codes.

With the end of the Knights Templar, so this theory goes, all evidence of the bloodline of Jesus disappeared from view for over 500 years. It was only in 1885 that someone began to penetrate the mystery, a young priest named François Bérenger Saunière, who was assigned to the parish at Rennes-le-Chateau, an ancient walled town in the French Pyrenees.

Saunière began to restore the town's sixth-century church. As he did so, he found a series of parchments hidden inside a hollow pillar. These parchments included some genealogical information and a collection of ciphers and codes. Allegedly the secrets of these codes made Saunière a wealthy man and he later spent much of his money on commissioning strange new artefacts for the church.

THE PRIORY OF SION

With Saunière's death the trail once again went cold, only to be revived by a Frenchman named Pierre Plantard who wrote extensively about the mysteries of Rennes-le-Chateau. He claimed that knowledge of the descendants of Jesus had remained in the hands of a mysterious organization called the Priory of Sion, an ancient secret order that lay behind the Knights Templar and guarded their legacy. Notable members included Leonardo da Vinci and Isaac Newton.

Sadly, this exotic theory did not convince many historians, many of whom were amused to discover that Pierre Plantard had registered the Priory of Sion as his own organization. He had also transparently forged genealogical documents, allegedly discovered by Saunière, which appeared to demonstrate that Plantard himself was a direct descendant of the Merovingian Kings – and thus of Jesus Christ himself!

And if all that sounds like the stuff of best-selling fiction rather than history, author Dan Brown can only agree with you. This most entertaining but unlikely of conspiracy theories formed the basis of his global bestseller, *The Da Vinci Code*.

God's Banker:
The Death of Roberto Calvi

The death of Roberto Calvi, nicknamed "God's banker" because of his close links with the Vatican, shocked the world in 1982, when he was found hanging beneath Blackfriars Bridge in London. Initially, his death was seen as suicide, but it soon emerged that murder was a much more likely scenario. Disturbing evidence came to light when the case was investigated, for it appeared that Calvi's shady financial dealings not only involved Italy's largest private bank and a secret Italian Masonic organization but the Vatican itself. To this day, the complex plot involving the bank, the Freemasons and the Vatican continues to unravel and it is still unclear exactly what happened. However, there seems to be no doubt that the Vatican was politically and financially implicated in the scandal, whether directly or indirectly.

Shady dealings

At the time of his death, 62-year-old Calvi was a successful businessman, the chairman of Banco Ambrosiana in Milan. Over his career he had built the bank up from a small concern to a large international organization with a huge financial empire. However, in 1978 Banco Ambrosiana was investigated by the Bank of Italy and found to be guilty of illegally exporting billions of lire. Calvi went on the run, and the bank began to collapse.

Three years later, he was arrested, tried and sentenced to four years in prison. After a short period of detention he was released on bail pending an appeal, but he had other charges to answer as well. At the time of his murder he was also being investigated for making fraudulent deals in the United States with a Sicilian banker called Michele Sindona.

As the investigations continued it emerged that the Vatican had a shareholding in Banco Ambrosiana and that Calvi was closely linked to Archbishop Paul Marcinkus, the head of the Vatican Bank. Enormous sums of money had been siphoned off from Banco Ambrosiana into the so-called "Institute for Religious Works", headed by Marcinkus, and there was speculation that this money had gone to fund right-wing regimes in Latin America that were friendly to the United States government and the Vatican. Another player in this complex game was Licio Gelli, a former Nazi, who ran a Masonic lodge known as Propaganda Due, or P2. This secret organization had a membership of over 1,000 prominent politicians, businessmen, and criminals, who were all united in a spirit of anti-communism as well as being dedicated to

RIGHT: Roberto Calvi in a Milan Courtroom 1981, after spending three years on the run. Calvi was sentenced to four years in prison for fraud, but was released on bail to await an appeal.

the enhancement of their own personal wealth and power.

MURDER NOT SUICIDE

In 1998 Calvi's family caused his body to be exhumed and, four years later, the initial verdict of suicide was overturned. It transpired that Calvi had been found with five bricks in his pocket and his hands tied behind his back. Moreover, his neck showed no signs of damage and there were none of his own fingerprints on the bricks. All of this pointed to the fact that he had not committed suicide as a reaction to financial ruination, but had been cold-bloodedly murdered by his enemies in the world of high finance and organized crime.

The killing had all the hallmarks of a Mafia-style execution. Police in Rome and London began to track down several suspects. Pippo Calo, a prominent member of the Sicilian Mafia; Flavio Carboni, a businessman with many interests all over the world; Carboni's ex-girlfriend, Manuela Kleinzig; Ernesto Diotallevi, the leader of a criminal organization in Rome called the "Banda della Magliana"; and a Mafia financier named Francesco Di Carlo. On 18 April 2005, the City of London police force charged Calo, Carboni, Kleinzig and Diotallevi with the murder.

AN UNHOLY MOB

In recent years, it has been suggested that the real reason that Calvi was murdered was to prevent him from making known the links between the Vatican, the P2 Freemasons and the Mafia. During his time at Banco Ambrosiana, enormous sums of money were transferred into the Vatican's coffers, resulting in the ultimate bankruptcy of Ambrosiana and its shareholders. (The day before Calvi died, his secretary Teresa Corrocher committed suicide by jumping out of a high window at the bank's headquarters. She left a note blaming her boss.)

It seems that Calvi and Gelli were in league. Calvi had been passing money from Ambrosiano and the Vatican Bank to Gelli and others, who in turn were busy negotiating political deals such as the sale of the Exocet missile from France to Argentina. In the view of many critics, the Vatican acted as a country with right-wing political interests, bankrolling whatever initiatives seemed beneficial to the Pope and the Catholic church, whether in Latin America or Europe. This was done secretly, with no regard whatsoever to democratic or sovereign rights in those countries. Obviously, if any of this information came out, it would be highly damaging to the Pope and the Vatican, who liked to preserve an image of being above politics.

THE DEATH OF JOHN PAUL I

When John Paul I took office as Pope in 1978, it looked as though some of the activities of Archbishop Marcinkus and the "Institute for Religious Works" would have to come to an end. However, John Paul I died only thirty-three days after his election, apparently of a heart attack. Some suspected foul play and indeed there were a number of anomalies surrounding the death, which was not well handled by the Vatican health carers. The Vatican press office also made many errors in reporting the death. In keeping with Vatican law, no post-mortem was performed on the Pope, which also caused some commentators to question what had happened. A controversy ensued, with some claiming that the Pope had been murdered and others holding the opposite view. For example, in his book, *In God's Name*, David Yallop suggested that

the Pope had been in danger the moment he took office. John Cornwell rejected this theory in his own book, *A Thief in the Night*, claiming that the Pope died as the result of a pulmonary embolism. He further suggested that the Vatican had acted in an incompetent, rather than a criminal, manner both during and after the tragedy. Whatever the truth of the matter, it seems that in terms of its political and financial dealings in the 1970s and 1980s, the Vatican had a great deal to hide. To this day, we still do not know the full extent of its involvement in the Calvi affair. Perhaps the ongoing trial will finally reveal the truth.

ABOVE: THE VIEW OF BLACKFRIARS BRIDGE IN LONDON, WHERE THE BODY OF ROBERTO CALVI WAS FOUND HANGING, JUNE 20TH 1982.

Skull and Bones

How is this for a coincidence? During the 2004 United States presidential elections both candidates – the incumbent, George W. Bush, and the Democratic challenger, John Kerry – were members of the same tiny secret society. The society in question is called Skull and Bones. It is based at Yale University and members are forbidden to speak about it at all. This was may have been modelled on the Illuminati society that flourished briefly in Germany some fifty years earlier.

It was this experience that inspired Russell, along with his friend Alphonso Taft, to start Skull and Bones. Some believe that the society was intended to be an American branch of the Illuminati. Others, more prosaically, suspect that it

When questioned regarding their membership of skull and bones, both Kerry and Bush replied: "It's a secret".

clearly evinced when both Bush and Kerry were quizzed about their membership by NBC's Meet the Press. NBC's interviewer, Tim Russert, asked both candidates about their membership and their answers were strikingly similar. "It's so secret we can't talk about it," said President Bush. "Not much, because it's a secret," said Kerry.

So what is known about this mysterious and evidently very powerful society? Skull and Bones was founded in 1832 by a Yale student named William H. Russell. Russell was the scion of a wealthy family who had made their fortune from the opium trade. Before attending Yale, Russell had spent time in Germany where he is believed to have been introduced to a secret society – one that

was just a reaction to Russell and Taft being denied membership of the prestigious Phi Beta Kappa fraternity.

Secret societies were much disapproved of in the United States at the time. President John Quincy Adams in particular had warned against the evils of Freemasonry. However, these clandestine organizations have always held a strong attraction and Skull and Bones proved to be no exception.

The secrets of the tomb

By 1856 the society was flourishing to the extent that it was able to build its own headquarters – an extraordinary, windowless, mausoleum-like building, known to society members as the Tomb.

ABOVE: SENATOR JOHN KERRY (L) AND U.S. PRESIDENT GEORGE W. BUSH SHAKE HANDS AT THE
CONCLUSION OF THEIR FIRST PRESIDENTIAL DEBATE AT THE UNIVERSITY OF MIAMI IN CORAL GABLES,
FLORIDA, 30 SEPTEMBER, 2004.

By then the society even had its own holding company, the Russell Trust Association, to look after its investments. It had also established the membership structure that remains to this day. Each year fifteen of the most brilliant (or well connected) are selected or "tapped" by senior Bonesmen, as they are called. Before long, this came to be seen as a great honour.

And it is not hard to see why. A list of the past members of Skull and Bones came to light in the 1980s, which revealed that its members included members of America's wealthiest and most powerful dynasties – Whitney, Adams, Rockefeller, etc. – alongside such renowned names as US President William Taft, political commentator William F. Buckley, Time-Life founder Henry Luce, poet Archibald MacLeish and Morgan Stanley founder Harold Stanley.

Three generations of Bushes are also on the list. Not just the current president's father, former president George H.W. Bush, but also his grandfather, Senator Prescott Bush. It was Prescott Bush who is alleged to have stolen one of the most prized of the many grisly treasures that are kept in the Tomb – the skull of Geronimo, personally grave-robbed for the society. It is alleged that the tomb also contains Hitler's silverware and that this is used for ceremonial dinners.

But it is not only high-profile figures who are Skull and Bones members. More often than not they are influential, but not well-known, people in the judiciary, the government and the CIA. In fact, the Skull and Bones are a gift for the conspiracy theorists. If you read that the Illuminati, say, had been involved in the development of the atomic bomb and its eventual use, had been leading figures in the post-war occupation of Germany, had played a leading role in post-war United States foreign policy and had substantial representation on little-known but powerful bodies like the Council on Foreign Relations and the Trilateral Commission, you'd take it with a pinch of salt. In the case of Skull and Bones, though, it is verifiably true.

On the other hand, some will argue, there is nothing surprising about the fact that a number of powerful people all belong to the same club. After all, doesn't that just indicate that they were the brightest and best at an elite university? Such people would naturally go on to run the country, of course.

SEXUAL HISTORY

Not so, say the conspiracy theorists, pointing to the bizarre bonding rituals and obsessive secrecy of the Skull and Bones crew. Their bonding rituals include lying in coffins and telling your fellow initiates your entire sexual history, thereby potentially laying yourself open to blackmail. And the secrecy itself inevitably invites suspicion – not to mention the financial support the Skull and Bones offers to its members or the private island in the Hudson River that is kept exclusively for the use of members. How does all that square with the

ABOVE: THE TEMPLE AT YALE, ALLEGEDLY USED BY THE SECRET
SKULL AND BONES SOCIETY FOR ITS RITUALS.

democratic ideals of America?

Some have been minded to compare the Skull and Bones oath of secrecy with the Mafia's code of omerta. However, as leading Skull and Bones expert Ron Rosenbaum has pointed out, "I think Skull and Bones has had slightly more success than the mafia in the sense that the leaders of the five mafia families are all doing 100 years in jail, while the leaders of the Skull and Bones families are doing four and eight years in the White House."

THE PROTOCOLS OF THE ELDERS OF ZION

The document known as The Protocols Of The Elders Of Zion is one of the earliest, most successful and enduring of all conspiracy theories. First circulated in Russia during the early twentieth century it purports to be a kind of manual for world domination that was written by a mysterious cabal of Jewish elders. It was then used to fuel fears that there was an international Jewish conspiracy that sought to take over the world. So successful was it in its aims that it has been used again and again over the ensuing century. Wherever there has been a rush of anti-Semitism, from Hitler's Germany to the training camps of Al-Qaeda, you can guarantee that a copy of The Protocols Of The Elders Of Zion will never be hard to find.

The document may only have appeared in its currently recognized form in the final years of Tsarist Russia, but it has its roots in the mid-nineteenth century. The story begins with a French popular novel called *The Mysteries Of The People*, written by Eugène Sue, which featured a group of Jesuits that were plotting to take over the world. This notion of a massive conspiracy was then taken up by the French satirist Maurice Joly, who used it in an 1864 pamphlet titled "Dialogues in Hell Between Machiavelli and Montesquieu", which attacked the political ambitions of the then French ruler, Napoleon III. This time,

however, the plotters, as the title suggests, were operating from beyond the grave.

Then, in 1868, Hermann Goedsche, a German anti-Semite and spy, wrote a book named *Biarritz*. This included a chapter entitled "The Jewish Cemetery in Prague and the Council of Representatives of the Twelve Tribes of Israel". The chapter described an imaginary secret rabbinical cabal meeting which was held in the cemetery at midnight every hundred years to plan the agenda for the Jewish Conspiracy. The set-up was plainly taken from an Alexandre Dumas novel, while the supposed secret agenda was actually straight from Joly's "Dialogues in Hell...".

SECRET POLICE

However, turning the supposed conspirators from Jesuits or dead philosophers into Jews touched a nerve and by the 1890s copies of this chapter of Goedsche's book, now treated as fact rather than fantasy or satire, were starting to circulate in Russia. Before long the Tsar's secret police, the Okhrana, recognized the potential popularity of the material and one of their operatives, Matvei Golovinski, worked up a book-length version of this fantastical Zionist plot. The book, now known as The Protocols Of The Elders Of Zion, was widely circulated and was undoubtedly influential in inflaming the anti-Jewish

ABOVE: VLADIMIR LENIN PREACHES TO THE MASSES, RUSSIA 1917. THE FACT THAT SOME BOLSHEVIK LEADERS WERE JEWISH WAS TAKEN BY MANY AS PROOF OF THE WORLDWIDE JEWISH CONSPIRACY.

pogrom that swept Russia in 1905–1906.

Curiously, one of the visions put forward by the Protocols – that of a small group taking over a huge country – was repeated by the real events of a decade later when the 1917 Bolshevik Revolution transformed Russia. Before long this was seen by many as evidence that the Bolshevik revolution was in fact part of the Jewish conspiracy. Jews and communists were now bracketed together across much of the world and the Protocols were put forward as damning evidence. The Protocols were popular with right wing elements in 1920s Germany and also in the United States. No less a man than Henry Ford sponsored the printing of half

a million copies in America.

Then the debunking began. Experts looked at the document and soon noticed that its origins lay in pulp fiction rather than historical fact. In 1920, one Lucien Wolf published an exposé tracing the history of the Protocols back to the works of Goedsche and Joly. The *Times* soon followed suit and, later that year, a book documenting the hoax was published in the United States by Herman Bernstein.

ADOLF HITLER

One might have thought that this would have been the end of the tale. Sadly not. By the 1920s anti-Semitism was endemic, nowhere more so than in Germany. Adolf

ABOVE: SENIOR MEMBERS OF THE NAZI PARTY, INCLUDING JULIUS STREICHER (L), AT A RALLY, 1935. ANTI-SEMITISM WAS THE CORNERSTONE OF THE NAZI WORLD VIEW.

Hitler referred to the Protocols in *Mein Kampf*: "To what extent the whole existence of this people is based on a continuous lie is shown incomparably by the Protocols of the Wise Men of Zion, so infinitely hated by the Jews", he wrote. He acknowledged the claims that the book was a forgery but ignored them, claiming instead that "with positively terrifying certainty they reveal the nature and activity of the Jewish people and expose their inner contexts as well as their ultimate final aims."

Once the Nazis took power in Germany the book became a set text in schools and helped fuel all the horrors of the Holocaust. It did not matter to the German Nazis that in 1934 a Swiss Nazi was brought to court after he had published a series of articles accepting the Protocols as fact. The trial, known as the Berne Trial, finished in May 1935 when the court declared the Protocols to be forgeries, plagiarisms and obscene literature. As far

as Hitler was concerned, however, a lurid lie beat the truth every time and the Swiss verdict was completely ignored.

The palpable falsity of the Protocols has not stopped their circulation in more recent times, either. They are widely published across the Arab world and have proved particularly popular in Iran, Egypt and Saudi Arabia, where they have been used to inflame opinion over the whole Palestinian question. In America, too, the Protocols are still accepted as fact by both neo-Nazi organizations and Louis Farrakhan's Nation Of Islam, which has distributed copies.

The history of the Protocols demonstrates that a powerful conspiracy theory need not have any factual basis to gain acceptance: it also reminds us that false conspiracy theories can do an enormous amount of harm if they are cynically used to back up the worst political objectives and to persecute innocent people.

THE GEMSTONE FILES

One of the most outrageous and entertaining global conspiracy theories is that of the mysterious Gemstone Files. This theory in essence suggests that the Mafia, led for a time by Aristotle Onassis, controlled America during the 1950s and 1960s.

Allegedly, the original Gemstone files were compiled from a series of writings and talks given by a man named Bruce Roberts in San Francisco during the late sixties and early seventies. The mysterious Roberts was supoosedly responsible for inventing the synthetic ruby used in laser technology, but claimed to have been swindled out of his discovery by the Howard Hughes organisation. He also claimed to have been involved in, or have knowledge of, a whole range of intelligence operations. He frequented a San Francisco pub called the Drift Inn where he would entertain his fellow regulars – including ex-intelligence agents – with improbable stories of outlandish secrets. Some of these may have been recorded and transcribed by the pub landlord. Others were written down by Roberts himself. Collected together, they run to over a thousand pages.

It's hard to know for sure, though, as very few, if any people, have ever seen the original manuscript. Instead what people have read is something called the *Skeleton Key To the Gemstone File*, a thirty-page summary of the original produced by one Stephanie Caruana, who was introduced to the original by a conspiracy theorist called Mae Brussell. All of this is hard to check because the mysterious Roberts allegedly died of cancer in 1975, and Mae Brussell died in 1988. As for the original files, according to another conspiracy theorist named Bill Keith, who has written a book about them, there are only four or five photocopies in existence and the owners refuse to part with them.

ONASSIS THE MAFIA BOSS!

So what we are left with is Caruana's *Skeleton Key*. This document was first hinted at in an article Caruana wrote for *Playgirl* magazine (of all the unlikely places for a sensational journalistic expose). Then, in 1974, she began to circulate Xeroxes of the Skeleton Key itself. These were copied and re-copied by conspiracy enthusiasts around the world. Partly because most copies looked illicit, the document soon gained an underground reputation.

So what was in the Gemstone Files, according to this *Skeleton Key*? Essentially, it is an impressionistic alternative history of the post-war era, one that weaves links between the CIA, FBI, and the Mafia, and seeks to explain the deaths of JFK, LBJ and Martin Luther King. Along the way, it brings in Ted Kennedy, Richard Nixon and San Francisco's Mayor Joe Alioto. At the heart of the conspiracy are two shadowy figures, Howard Hughes and Aristotle Onassis.

According to the Gemstone Files, Onassis was a drug dealer who made his fortune selling opium to Turkey before going into partnership with Joe Kennedy (JFK's father) to smuggle booze into the USA during prohibition. By the 1950s, Onassis was running the Mafia. Meanwhile, the Texan millionaire Howard Hughes was buying up politicians with a view to controlling the Presidency.

Onassis saw Hughes as a rival, kidnapped him and replaced him with a double (which explains why Hughes became a recluse in his later years). Now Onassis controlled both the Mafia and a number of key politicians. In the 1960 election both candidates, Kennedy and Nixon, were beholden to him – so either way, he won.

However, when Kennedy pulled back from invading Cuba, the Mafia decided to have him killed. And so on, and so on.

ABOVE: JACQUELINE KENNEDY ONASSIS ACCOMPANIES HER HUSBAND, ARISTOTLE, TO A PLANE AT KENNEDY AIRPORT, ANOTHER KENNEDY-ONASSIS CONNECTION.

ABOVE: MEYER LANSKY, ONE-TIME PARTNER OF 'LUCKY' LUCIANO. LANSKY, LIKE MANY IN THE MAFIA, HAD BIG INVESTMENTS IN CUBA, AND WAS SEVERELY AFFECTED BY CASTRO'S TAKEOVER OF THE ISLAND.

Every assassination during the sixties could be laid at the feet of this sinister conspiracy. Particularly bizarre are the allegations that Onassis kept the real Howard Hughes prisoner on his private Greek island and only married Jackie Kennedy as part of his revenge on the treacherous JFK.

FROM GEMSTONES TO X-FILES

All in all, Onassis emerges more as a Bond super-villain than a real person. And that may be the key to the Gemstone Files' enduring popularity. This is the Bond movie version of modern history – more colourful and exciting than real life could ever be. And, in turn, the kind of conspiracy theories propounded in the Gemstone Files have definitely influenced many movies: they notions inform Oliver Stone's films like *JFK* and *Nixon*, and have also influenced TV shows like the *X-Files*.

So do the Gemstone Files have any serious credibility at all? Well, some of the many theories that are bandied about in their pages do bear consideration. That there was some kind of connection between JFK and the Mafia, for instance, seems certain. Overall though, the Files are clearly written by someone who had a few nuggets of inside knowledge, but proceeded to put two and two together and make a million. As for whether the real author was the mysterious Roberts, or whether Brussell or Caruana was actually the author of the Files, remains open to speculation. Whoever the author was, though, the Gemstone Files are ultimately an entertaining and remarkably influential work of fiction.

CHAPTER THREE:

ALTHOUGH NINETEENTH-CENTURY AUTHORS SUCH AS
JULES VERNE SPECULATED ON THE SUBJECT OF ALIEN
LIFE-FORMS, IT WAS NOT UNTIL THE SECOND HALF OF
THE TWENTIETH CENTURY THAT THE EXISTENCE OF
BEINGS FROM OTHER WORLDS BECAME SUCH A

THE UNKNOWN

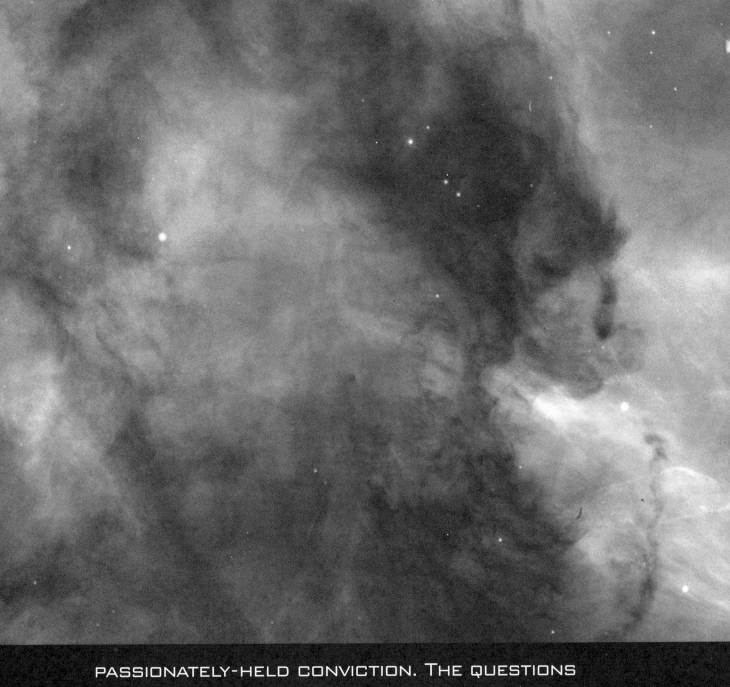

PASSIONATELY-HELD CONVICTION. THE QUESTIONS
REMAIN: DO SUCH LIFE-FORMS EXIST, HAVE THEY
TRAVELLED MILLIONS OF LIGHT YEARS TO VISIT US, AND
ARE GOVERNMENTS OF THE WORLD IN COLLUSION TO
COVER UP THESE VISITS?

Flying Saucers: The Roswell Incident

The Roswell Incident of June 1947 remains one of the most intriguing episodes in the history of UFO research. For many, it is the most persuasive evidence we have that alien beings exist, that they travel about the cosmos in spacecraft and that they once landed here on Earth.

The story began in 1947 when a pilot named Kenneth Arnold claimed that he had seen several objects flying "like geese" through the sky near Mount Rainier, Washington. He described them "moving like a saucer would if it skimmed across the water". The journalist reporting the story coined the term "flying saucer" to describe the craft and this has been used informally ever since to denote UFOs – unidentified flying objects.

Whether such objects exist, and whether Arnold was telling the truth when he made the claim that day, has been the subject of much speculation over the years. For what happened a few weeks afterwards confirmed, in many people's minds, that aliens had indeed visited our planet and that the American government, for reasons of its own, tried to hush up the story.

Extra-terrestrial crash landing?

In early July 1947, a rancher named William "Mack" Brazel was riding out over land near Corona, New Mexico when he noticed a large amount of strange-looking debris scattered about. He informed Sheriff Wilcox of Chaves County who, thinking this must be to do with military exercises, passed the information on to the Army Air Force base at Roswell. Major Jesse Marcel, the base intelligence officer, was instructed to examine the debris. Meanwhile, a local newspaper published the story, reporting that a "flying saucer" had landed on the ranch (they also claimed that it had "been captured", which was a complete fabrication). The matter was then referred to the United States Army Air Force research laboratories, who issued a statement to the effect that the debris was not a flying saucer but the remains of a high altitude weather balloon with a radar attachment made of aluminium and balsa wood, that was being used for State purposes.

After the sighting in New Mexico, the press picked up the story and many newspapers across the United States published more or less lurid accounts of it. Public interest ran high and various other sightings were reported during the summer of 1947. However, the Army's insistence that the wreckage was not a crashed or captured flying saucer but simply the remains of a weather balloon eventually began to quell press and public interest in the subject.

THE EVIDENCE

The Roswell Incident, as it came to be called, looked destined to slip into obscurity for many years, but in 1978 a UFO researcher named Stanton Friedman began to delve into it once again. While on a lecture tour, he received a call from Jesse Marcel, who had handled the affair back in 1947. However, Marcel could not remember the date on which the incident took place. With the help of co-researcher William Moore, Friedman began to find out more and eventually unearthed newspaper clippings reporting the story. Then the pair began to ask questions. What kind of weather balloon could yield such strange debris? Brazel and others had said that the material they had found

U Daily Record

RECORD PHONE
Business Office 22
News Department
2287

ROSWELL, NEW MEXICO,   TUESDAY, JULY 8 1947

RAAF Captures Flying Sauce
On Ranch in Roswell Regior

House Passes Tax Slash by Large Margin

Defeat Amendment By Demos to Remove Many from Rolls

Washington, July 8 (AP) — The house passed today the Republican-backed bill to cut income taxes by $4,000,000,000 annually for 49,000,000 taxpayers, beginning Jan. 1.

It goes to the senate where approval also is forecast.

The vote was 302 to 11, or more than the two-thirds majority needed to override a presidential veto.

The action, which may encounter another presidential veto, came after Speaker Martin (R-Mass.), personally appeal to the house to pass the bill by such a decisive vote—as to persuade the president that the people should have this delayed justice."

The measure is identical with one vetoed by President Truman June 16 as "the wrong kind of tax reduction at the wrong time"—except that the effective date is changed from July 1, 1947 to Jan. 1, 1948.

Congress leaders expect to have the revised bill on Mr. Truman's desk before the week ends.

The house passed the bill after the Republicans beat back a proposed Democratic substitute that would have reduced taxes by $3,379,000,000 and removed 4,000,000 low-income persons from the tax rolls completely.
——0——

Security Council Paves Way to Talks On Arms Reductions

Lake Success, July 8 (AP) — The United Nations security council today approved an American blueprint for arms reduction discussions despite a Russian warning that the plan would bring about a collapse of arms regulation efforts.

The vote was 9 to 0, with Russian and Poland abstaining.

In view of Russia's firm stand against the U. S. plan it had been believed she might invoke the big power veto to block it.

Soviet Deputy Foreign Minister Andrei A. Gromyko gave his warning before the United Nations security council in a new effort to revive the Soviet working plan which already had been rejected by the commission for conventional armaments.

His challenge was taken up promptly by French delegate Alexandre Parodi and U. S. Representative Herschel V. Johnson, who announced their opposition to any substitute for the American plan.

Gromyko insisted that no program for arms regulation could succeed unless the plan was linked directly with an absolute prohibition of atomic weapons.

He declared that the U. S. plan approved by the commission did not link the problems of arms reduction and the banning of atomic weapons and, for this reason, it offered no basis for a solution.

Gromyko opened debate on the arms question as delegates awaited another major declaration from him later in the day in reply to United States and British demands for action to restore order in the

No Details of Flying Disk Are Revealed

Roswell Hardware Man and Wife Report Disk Seen

The intelligence office of the 509th Bombardment group at Roswell Army Air Field announced at noon today, that the field has come into possession of a flying saucer.

According to information released by the department, over authority of Maj. J. A. Marcel, intelligence officer, the disk was recovered on a ranch in the Roswell vicinity, after an unidentified rancher had notified Sheriff Geo. Wilcox, here, that he had found the instrument on his premises.

Major Marcel and a detail from his department went to the ranch and recovered the disk, it was stated.

After the intelligence office here had inspected the instrument it was flown to "higher headquarters."

The intelligence office stated that no details of the saucer's construction or its appearance had been revealed.

Mr. and Mrs. Dan Wilmot apparently were the only persons in Roswell who have seen what they thought was a flying disk.

They were sitting on their porch at 105 South Penn. last Wednesday night at about ten minutes before ten o'clock when a large glowing object zoomed out of the sky from the southeast, going in a northwesterly direction at a high rate of speed.

Ex-King Carol Weds Mme. Lupescu

Former King Carol of Romania and Mme. Elena Lu relax aboard the S. S. America bound for Cuba and Mex May, 1941. A member of Carol's household in Rio de Ja said the ex-king and his companion for 23 years in reig exile were recently married at their hotel Copacabana F suite. (AP Wirephoto).

Miners and Operators Sign
Highest Wage Pact in Histo

called a meeting to talk it

ABOVE: THE STORY THAT LAUNCHED A THOUSAND SAUCERS: THE *DAILY RECORD* OF 8 JULY 1947 REPORTS THE ROSWELL 'INCIDENT'.

was extremely light and could not be burned or otherwise destroyed. Why would they lie about such a thing? And why was the whole affair cloaked in such secrecy? The Army seemed to have something to hide – what was it?

LITTLE GREEN MEN

Friedman and Moore interviewed a teletype operator named Lydia Sleppy. She had worked at a New Mexico radio station in 1947 and had claimed that the FBI had interrupted the transmission of the "flying saucer" story. This seemed to tally with Marcel's account, in which he had stated that the army had suppressed information about the strange debris that he had seen with his own eyes and that the "weather balloon" story had been a cover up. A retired Air Force brigadier general called Arthur Exon then came out of the woodwork. He told UFO researchers Kevin Randle and Donald Schmitt that some strange debris had been brought in while he had been working at the Wright Patterson Air Force Base in 1947. It was lightweight and apparently indestructible. There were also rumours circulating around the base, he said, that bodies had been recovered out of a "craft from space".

Another retired Air Force officer, Brigadier General Thomas Dubose, alleged in interviews that the Roswell incident had been treated with the greatest secrecy and that the White House had been involved. He also confirmed that the "weather balloon" story had been

fabricated. Other senior ex-officers then emerged with similar tales to tell: they had either seen the bodies of alien creatures who had died when the craft crashed or they had heard of their existence.

Much of this evidence was dismissed by sceptics as second hand. Yet there remained disturbing anomalies in the government's weather balloon story, so – not surprisingly – questions continued to be asked.

SECRET SURVEILLANCE?

Several theories were advanced. The first, and in the opinion of many people, the most persuasive, was that the debris was surveillance equipment that was being used in a top secret government project designed to spy on Russian nuclear activity, called Mogul. The incident needed to be hushed up because of the clandestine nature of the operation, which is why the army came up with the story about the weather balloon. However, this theory does not explain why the material found on the ranch was so unusual, or why the army would be using such material. It was also pointed out that the army had previously been unconcerned about people stumbling across the evidence of balloons and other army equipment found scattered in the desert: but this time they rushed to hide it.

Next came the idea that the incident could be attributed to a nuclear accident on the part of the army but, once again, there were problems with this explanation. For a start, the army had no assembled

ABOVE : AREA 51 IS STILL A RESTRICTED SITE, A FACT POINTED OUT BY CONSPIRACY THEORISTS WHO BELIEVE THE GOVERNMENT HAS SOMETHING TO HIDE.

nuclear weapons in its arsenal at the time and there were no other nuclear accidents during the period in question, as public records now attest. Critics also argued that if the army had lost a nuclear weapon in the desert they would surely not have waited for a passing rancher to let them know where it was!

So what really happened?

Because of the government secrecy surrounding the issue, a number of UFO researchers have come to the conclusion that some kind of covert activity must have taken place. Some believe that there was an alien landing and that the United States government simply denied the fact in order to prevent panic among the public. Others suggest that the government has access to alien technology but refuses to admit it. There

has even been speculation that this was either a crash between two alien spacecraft or a crash involving a spy craft which secretly experimented on live human beings. This latter theory, advanced by Nick Redfern in his book *Body Snatchers in the Desert*, has gained credibility within the UFO field, if not outside it.

Ultimately, it seems that right up to this day nobody really knows what took place. Even the most persuasive theories that have been advanced appear to be full of loose ends. However, whether or not we believe that alien beings landed in the desert that day, what we do know is that there was a lot more to the incident than a burst weather balloon. And that is why, for the foreseeable future, UFO researchers and others will continue to ask: what really happened at Roswell?

THE RENDLESHAM AFFAIR

In the early hours of Boxing Day, 1980, a strange incident occurred in Rendlesham Forest, Suffolk. Close to the pine forest was an American Air Force Base, which suddenly began to track an unidentified craft on its radar. The base was immediately put on full alert, but after a while it became clear that the craft was not aggressive and that there was no real threat. However, a patrol was sent to the forest to investigate. After the patrol had reached the site by following a dark, narrow path the men saw bright beams of red and blue light shining from what appeared to be a metallic craft that had landed in the forest. Other craft hovered silently in the sky above.

TRANCE-LIKE STATE

Base Commander Gordon Williams reported that he approached the craft on the ground and communicated with the creatures in it through sign language. Other witnesses told of watching the creatures repair their craft, which had become damaged when it crashed in the forest, and then take off in a huge burst of speed and light.

After the craft had left, the airmen said that they had found themselves in a trance-like state so that general confusion prevailed. Local people also reported that their farm animals and domestic pets had become disorientated and panic-stricken, to the extent that they had been running out on to the roads and colliding with

vehicles. There were also accounts that flickering blue and red lights played over the trees throughout the rest of the night. Some people even said that small creatures with domed heads had been seen wandering through the forest.

EVIDENCE OF ALIENS

Because of the airmen's confused condition at the time, it was difficult to verify exactly what had happened. However, the indisputable fact was that a very strange occurrence had taken place in the forest, one that could not easily be explained. On the next day, forensic tests were carried out over the whole site and some odd facts emerged.

Firstly, there were some marks on the ground where the landing legs of the craft were thought to have been. These gave out very high levels of radiation. Secondly, the treetops in the area had been damaged as though an aeroplane or other large object had crashed through them. And thirdly, a tape recording of the search had been made by an airman at the time and there were strange noises on it.

To this day, why the radiation levels on the site went up and why the trees in the vicinity were damaged remains a mystery. However, some have disputed the veracity of this tape, claiming that it is a hoax.

RIGHT: DAMAGED TREES IN RENDLESHAM FOREST, ENGLAND, THE SITE OF ALLEGED ALIEN LANDINGS TESTIFIED TO BY US SERVICE PERSONNEL. IN FACT, THE 'HOVERING LIGHT' THEY SAW WAS MORE LIKELY TO HAVE BEEN THE LOCAL LIGHTHOUSE.

Since the incident, it has also been rumoured that a video recording of the whole event exists. It was supposedly made by one of the airmen who witnessed it from start to finish. Because this material was so sensitive, it is thought that the military confiscated it and that it then became classified information, never to be made public.

Conspiracy theory?

Many believe that the hushing up of the incident was a conspiracy by the United States military, who were attempting to

cover up the fact that there had been a nuclear accident at Rendlesham. In order to avoid local panic, and to deflect criticism, the personnel at the air base pretended that some kind of alien landing had taken place. Other commentators have put forward the theory that the event was actually an American attack on a Russian spy satellite and that it was the satellite, not an alien craft, that was brought down in the forest.

Various other conspiracy theories have been put forward. It has been suggested that the strange craft were top secret air force aerospace vehicles, known as TR-3Bs or "Astras". Inside each of these huge

ABOVE: US STEALTH BOMBER. BLACK, TRIANGULAR AND EXTREMELY FAST AND MANOEVRABLE, COULD THESE AIRCRAFT BE THE SOURCE OF UFO SIGHTINGS?

vehicles, it is said, is a nuclear reactor that negates the Earth's magnetic field, so that the craft becomes very light. It can then move quickly and flexibly within the magnetic field it has created. In addition to the "Astras" there are smaller craft with similar capabilities, so the story goes, called TR-3As or "Black Mantas". Critics of this theory have pointed out that it would be very difficult to house a nuclear reactor in this way, because it would be extremely heavy. This has then given rise to another theory, that the United States military is in possession of alien technology.

OTHER SIGHTINGS

There are many other well-documented sightings of "black triangle" UFOs such as the one that is believed to have landed at Rendlesham Forest in 1980. Most of these have been seen in and around the coast of the United States, particularly near air force bases. According to reports, the UFOs are hundreds of feet long, they make no sound and they either hover or fly very rapidly. One of the most significant of these sightings was at Ans, in Belgium, where on 30 March 1990 the local citizens reported seeing a hovering black triangle over the city. Members of the Belgian Air Force pursued the craft but were not able to keep up with it. They later issued a report admitting that they could not identify the phenomenon. Similarly, on 13 March 1997 in Phoenix, Arizona, citizens noticed "black triangle" craft forming a "V" in the sky. Later, the Air Force reported

COULD THE BLACK TRIANGLES, AS SOME HAVE SUGGESTED, BE VISITATIONS FROM EXTRA-TERRESTRIAL BEINGS?

that what people had seen were flare tests, but this seemed highly unlikely.

Today, the consensus seems to be that such aircraft do actually exist. The Belgian Air Force has evidence of the "black triangle" aircraft that visited Ans that day in the shape of radar tracking, photographs and film. What we still do not know, however, is where the craft come from, who they belong to, how they function and why they appear. Could the black triangles, as some suggest, be evidence of top-secret, advanced US military technology? Are they perhaps signs from an underground, possibly terrorist group, who want to display their might in this way? Or could they indeed be visitations from extra-terrestrial beings? At present, and for the foreseeable future, the mystery remains.

CROP CIRCLES: ALIEN VISITORS OR LOCAL HOAXERS?

The mysterious appearance of circular patterns in cornfields first hit the headlines during the 1970s, when several of them appeared in England. After these sightings, many people around the world began to report the occurrence of curious, and in some cases very beautiful, patterns in paddy fields and pine forests as well as on snow-covered hills. Critics immediately dismissed the circles as hoaxes and, indeed, some individuals came forward claiming that they had made the circles as a prank.

However, on closer inspection, it became clear that the phenomenon could not be explained so easily. Many aspects of it were very puzzling. For example, the circles typically appeared rapidly; their patterns were complex and very accurate, as though drawn by a compass; and the biological structure of the plants that formed them had changed. Eminent scientists began to conduct research into crop circles and they came up with numerous theories as to how such phenomena could occur. For example, magnetic fields and different types of geological formation could be affecting the plants, causing them to flatten and change.

Yet, to date, no one has come up with a conclusive theory that explains how crop circles have come about. The popular belief that they are evidence of extra-terrestrial beings, perhaps messages to humanity from a higher intelligence on a different planet, continues to predominate.

THE FIRST CROP CIRCLES

Within the ancient folklore of Britain and Northern Europe can be found stories of circles in grass or cornfields. They were thought to be caused by elves and fairies and they could cause disaster if people trod on them. A sixteenth-century woodcut shows a picture of a monstrous creature making a circle in a corn field. However, there are various interpretations of the image and it could well refer to an entirely imaginary event. The first scientific evidence did not appear until the twentieth century, when aerial surveys revealed what were then termed "crop marks" which were thought to be caused by changes in the soil. Many of the sites were investigated and archaeological finds were made, but little attention was paid to the "crop marks" themselves.

FLYING SAUCERS

It was not until 1972 that two men, Arthur Shuttlewood and Bryce Bond, reported seeing a crop circle appear before them on a moonlit night at a place called Star Hill, near Warminster in England. They had come out to look for unidentified flying

ABOVE: CROP CIRCLE NEAR THE IRON AGE BURIAL MOUND OF SILBURY HILL IN WILTSHIRE, ENGLAND. ALTHOUGH THERE IS MUCH ANEDOTAL EVIDENCE FOR THE MYSTERIOUS PROPERTIES OF CROP CIRCLES, THERE IS VERY LITTLE THAT IS SCIENTIFICALLY VERIFIABLE.

objects, or UFOs, which had apparently been seen many times in the area over a period of ten years or so. Instead, an imprint on the vegetation suddenly materialized before their eyes, opening up like a fan.

After that, many witnesses from around the world, from Japan to the Soviet Union, came forward with similar stories. Apart from the circles, they also told of having seen aircraft and beams of light and heard a high trilling sound. Reported sightings of crop circles increased in number, until they reached the current figure of over 9,000. There are thought to be many more that go unreported each year.

Doug and Dave

Doug and Dave were pranksters who came forward to announce that they had created the crop circles. They claimed that all of them had been made using planks of wood, string and a baseball cap. However, as more complex patterns were reported it became clear that Doug and Dave could not possibly have made such complicated circles. Moreover, because reports were coming in from all over the world, it was hard to explain how they had been in so many places at the same time. In the end, Doug and Dave had to admit that they were not responsible for all the crop circles that were being reported.

GENUINE FORMATIONS

Once the formations had been looked at scientifically, it began to become clear that human beings could not possibly have made them. When plants from the circles were analyzed under the microscope, it was noticed that their biological structure had changed. Not only this, but nodes on the plant stems appeared to have been blown open in a way that was consistent with them having been heated up. In many cases, otherwise brittle stems were bent but not broken, something that would have been impossible for human beings to do by hand.

Another odd aspect of the formations was that they seemed to alter the magnetic field of the area, so that camera crews filming them suddenly discovered that their equipment was not working. Compasses, mobile phones and batteries also stopped working when they were close to the formations. Aircraft flying above them also reported equipment failure. People living in villages that were close to where circles appeared often told of power cuts, cars failing to start and animals refusing to walk across or near the circles.

WHAT CAUSES CIRCLES?

Most people prefer not to believe that little green aliens travelling around the planet in flying saucers are responsible for the happenings, so a variety of other

LEFT: CROP CIRCLES IN CALIFORNIA: CAROLYN NORTH, AUTHOR OF TWO BOOKS ON THE CROP CIRCLE PHENOMENON, STANDS IN THE CENTRE OF A CIRCLE TO SEE WHAT KIND OF ENERGY IS FELT.

explanations have been sought. Archaelogists, geologists and others have pointed to the fact that crop circles often occur over the Earth's magnetic energy lines, which are also known as ley lines. Early humankind often built structures in these places: Stonehenge is just one example. Recent thinking suggests that eddies in the Earth's magnetic field cause crops to flatten and that other environmental factors, such as underground water tables, may make the nodes of plant stems swell up as if heated.

However, this by no means accounts for the appearance of all crop circles, especially the very complex ones. There remains a great deal of controversy over whether the most spectacular crop circles occur naturally, whether they are the work of human beings or whether they are evidence of alien intervention. It is certainly true that many groups of artists and nature lovers make crop circles, either because they believe that they have a healing effect on the human psyche or because they feel that they are beautiful to look at. However, many have argued that such activity cannot account for every instance of the phenomenon.

Thus, until scientists come up with a completely persuasive explanation for the way in which crop circles suddenly appear on our landscape, enthusiasts will continue to believe that they are the result of supernatural forces. Not little green men, perhaps, but forms of life that, as yet, we know nothing about.

THE MEN IN BLACK

Who are the men in black? Legend has it that these elusive figures are a group of agents that materialize whenever an unidentified flying object appears or any other extraterrestrial occurrence takes place. Their task is to harass or frighten witnesses into denying all knowledge of what has happened. The conspiracy theory that lies behind the idea of the men in black is that alien beings are threatening our planet and want to hide the information from the public. Alternatively, it has been suggested that the men in black are government agents who also wish to suppress the truth.

According to the theory, the government agents or "MIBs" are usually dressed in black suits and display behaviour which is unusual and, possibly, non-human. They threaten witnesses and confiscate photographs, video tapes and anything other means of recording a sighting. In some cases, their black suits have been described as made of a strange shiny fabric which witnesses have not seen before. They have also been described as "mechanical", with monotonous voices and robotic movements. Some reports even attest to the fact that their faces are not like human faces but have odd slanted eyes and high cheekbones. They are said to travel in threes most of the time, but they have occasionally been reported as travelling alone.

MIBs, so the story goes, drive new Lincolns or Cadillacs, often with the headlights off, and the inside of the cars is lit with a strange green or purple light. The license plates of the cars are false and there are sometimes odd emblems on the doors. Occasionally, the MIBs arrive in black helicopters and tail witnesses of UFO happenings, intimidating them into giving up any evidence they might have.

FIRST SIGHTINGS

Since the earliest times, there have always been accounts of emissaries from the gods, or from devils, who disguise themselves to do their masters' business on Earth. In particular, demons were said to wear black, usually sporting the fashions of the day, and to ride about in black carriages in a similar way to the Men in Black of today's urban tales. An eighteenth-century Norwegian story tells of a young girl who was travelling with her grandmother to meet the devil (who turned out to be her grandfather!) and who, on the way, met three men dressed in black. Another, from the early twentieth century, tells of a religious cult that was centred around a woman named Mary Jones. Its members reported seeing strange lights in the sky and encountering "dread apparitions" in the night, including men dressed in black.

There has also been speculation among some ufologists that mythical figures from the past, such as Elizabethan and Native American "black men" or nineteenth-century evil travelling salesmen, could in fact have been "Men in Black" who were travelling the earth in order to silence those who had witnessed extraterrestrial events.

The first modern sighting, however, took place in 1947, when a sailor named Harold Dahl reported seeing six unidentified flying objects at a place called Maury Island near Tacoma, Washington. Dahl, who was with his son and his dog, took some photographs. His dog was reportedly killed when some hot sparks from the UFOs landed on the boat. Next day, a man called at his home and took him out to a diner for breakfast. The man, who was tall and dark and wearing a black suit, pumped him for details of the sighting and gave him a severe warning not to tell anyone of it – otherwise his family might be harmed. Later, Dahl claimed that the sighting was a hoax. This was apparently an attempt to follow the MIB's orders, but it caused some confusion and many began to doubt the veracity of his story.

ALBERT K. BENDER

One of the earliest people to pick up on the story was Albert K. Bender, director of the "International Flying Saucer Bureau" and editor of a UFO newsletter entitled *The Space Review*. In a 1953 article, Bender alleged that he had acquired information about flying saucers but was unable to print it and warned that anyone who had similar information was in danger. Issues of *The Space Review* then ceased. Later, Bender explained what had happened. He said that he had been visited by three men in dark suits who had told him the secrets of UFOs and then intimidated him into silence.

After Bender's story was made public, controversy arose around the question of whether or not the "Men in Black" story had been dreamed up by UFO enthusiasts to cover up the fact that they had very little evidence for their stories. Sceptics pointed out that having government or alien agents harass UFO witnesses into silence was a very handy device for explaining why concrete information was not forthcoming. The ufologists, such as writer Gray Barker, Bender's friend, countered by alleging that "sinister men" were suppressing the real story of what was going on in the extraterrestrial world.

MEN IN BLACK: TOMMY LEE JONES AND WILL SMITH CONFRONT AN ALIEN IN THE FILM OF THE SAME NAME.

Return of the Men in Black

In 1976, a visit from a "man in black" was reported in Maine, by Dr Herbert Hopkins, who had been told about a UFO sighting in the area. According to Hopkins, the man was dressed in a smart black suit but looked extremely strange, with a pale face and bright red lipstick. He threatened Hopkins in a slow, monotonous voice, telling him not to publicize the UFO encounter in any way. He then walked out, leaving Hopkins in a trance-like state.

Four years later there was another visit, this time to Peter Rojcewicz, a folklorist, while he was in the library at Pennsylvania University. A tall man with a dark face, dressed in a black suit, came up behind him and began to question him about his studies. Rojcewicz told the man that he was researching UFO encounters, whereupon the man became angry but then calmed down. After he left, Rojcewicz became panicky and went to find help, but there seemed to be nobody around. Later, he realized that there had been people in the library all along, but he had not been able to see them.

Who are the MIBs?

According to US government sources, there is some evidence to suggest that people who have witnessed UFO activity have sometimes been harassed. It is thought that ordinary members of the public have sometimes posed as government officials and intimidated witnesses. In one case, witness Rex Heflin of Santa Ana, California, took photographs of a UFO in 1965, which were published. He later told of receiving a visit from two men who claimed to be representatives of the North American Aerospace Defense Command. They asked for the negatives of the photographs and took them away, never to return them.

Although this case was well documented, there were thought to be many inconsistencies in Heflin's account and to date there is little concrete evidence to suggest that the Men in Black actually exist. One complicating factor is that those who claim to have been visited by them often report themselves to have been in a trance-like mental state both during the encounter and after it. This has led some commentators to believe that instead of having been visited by MIBs, the "witnesses" have actually been undergoing some kind of mental crisis which has impaired their state of mind, so that they imagined the whole event.

Another explanation, advanced by the pro-UFO lobby, is that government officials have in fact dressed up in strange clothes in order to discredit the stories of UFO witnesses. Others suggest that the MIBs are in fact alien-human hybrids whose job it is to cover up any trace of alien activity on Earth. Whatever the truth, it seems that these visits have a long history – whether as real events, or as stories that have moved from the folklore of the past to present-day urban mythology – and they look set to continue in the future.

THE MOON LANDINGS

It is one of the iconic images of the past century: Neil Armstrong emerging from Apollo 11 and uttering the immortal words "A small step for man, a giant step for mankind" – words so apt that they seemed to have been scripted. But what if the whole thing actually was scripted? What if the moon landings never really happened, but were mocked up in a film studio as a propaganda exercise?

That is precisely the belief of an increasing number of Americans. It is an apparently outlandish conspiracy theory that was ridiculed when it first appeared in the early 1970s but has slowly gained credence ever since. After Watergate,

BELOW: WALKING ON THE MOON: ONE OF THE APOLLO 12 ASTRONAUTS IS PHOTOGRAPHED WITH TOOLS AND CARRIER FOR LUNAR HAND TOOLS DURING MOONWALK ACTIVITIES.

Americans became immeasurably more cynical about their government. So when the 1978 film Capricorn One portrayed a NASA attempt to fake a landing on Mars, many were prompted to suspect that the film was actually based on inside information. Since then opinion polls have consistently indicated that millions of Americans have their doubts about the moon landings. These doubts were fanned by a Fox Documentary made in 2002, which gave the conspiracy theorists the chance to put their case.

Were the landings faked?

So what is that case? What is it about the moon landings, watched by millions at the time and for many years after seen as evidence of one of mankind's supreme achievements, that makes the conspiracy theorists suspicious?

Perhaps the best known questions posed by the conspiracy theorists are to do with the photographs of the landings. Why does the American flag appear to be waving in the wind when the moon has no wind? And why are there no stars visible in the sky? Not only that, why do photographs that purport to be taken miles apart appear to have identical backgrounds?

So what explanations can NASA, or anyone else, offer to explain these

LEFT: LIGHT AND SHADOW: THAT THE ASTRONAUT IS BRIGHTLY LIT WHEN HE IS STANDING IN THE SHADOW OF THE LANDER PROVES FOR MANY PEOPLE THE PRESENCE OF A SECOND LIGHT SOURCE – AN IMPOSSIBILITY ON THE MOON. THE EFFECT IS, HOWEVER, CAUSED BY THE REFLECTION OF LIGHT FROM THE GROUND.

apparent anomalies? Well, quite a few. Taking them in order: the flag is apparently waving because it had just been unwrapped and then twisted as the flagpole was screwed into the ground. The reason no stars are visible is because the cameras that were used were set for quick shutter speeds, in order not to over-expose the film in the very bright light. The dim light of the stars simply does not have a chance to show up on the film. This same effect can easily be observed on Earth. If you take a picture of the night sky with the camera set for a bright sunny day then the stars will be invisible. The allegation that the backgrounds are identical in different photographs does not stand up to detailed analysis either. A careful comparison of the backgrounds that are claimed to be identical in fact shows significant changes in the relative positions of the hills.

It is just the same on Earth, where a mountain range will appear in much the same place in the backgrounds of photographs taken several hundred feet apart.

Why no blast crater?

The photographs are just one set of issues that have been raised by the conspiracy theorists, however. Some of their other questions deal with more mechanical matters.

Why was there no blast crater visible following the lunar landings? Why did the launch rocket not produce a visible flame? How did the spaceship and its crew survive the journey through the Van Allen radiation belt?

Here are the official scientific responses. There was no blast crater for the simple reason that the Lunar Modules braked before landing, rather than crashing violently into the moon's surface. In any case, their impact was diminished by the much weaker gravity on the moon. There was no visible flame because the Lunar Module used hydrazine and dinitrogen tetroxide, propellants chosen for their ability to ignite upon contact and without a spark. Such propellants happen to produce a nearly transparent exhaust. As for the Van Allen belt, the mission was well prepared for this. The orbital transfer trajectory from the Earth to the Moon through the belts was selected to minimize radiation exposure so that the spacecraft moved through the belts in just thirty minutes. The astronauts were protected from the radiation by the metal hulls of the spacecraft. The dosage received by the astronauts was no more than that gained from a chest X-ray.

MOON ROCKS

Finally, one particularly complex part of the conspiracy theory has to do with the question of the moon rocks. These are usually seen as the ultimate proof that the moon landings did indeed take place. How else could these rocks, completely different to anything seen on Earth, have come in the possession of NASA? Conspiracy theorists point to the Antarctic expedition of Wernher von Braun, two

years prior to the Apollo mission. According to this theory, this mission was used to collect lunar meteorite rocks that could be used as fake moon rocks in a hoax. Von Braun was susceptible to pressure from the authorities. He would have agreed to the conspiracy in order to protect himself from recriminations over his past as a former Nazi.

Well it is a nice theory and it does have some scientific rationale. There are indeed lunar meteorites to be found in Antarctica. However, the first meteorite identified as a lunar meteorite was not found until 1981, over a decade after the moon landings. It was only identified as such because of its similarity to the lunar samples returned by Apollo, which in turn are similar to the few grams of material returned from the moon by Soviet sample return. The total collection of identified Antarctic lunar meteorites presently amounts to only about 2.5 kilograms, less than one per cent of the 381 kilograms of moon rocks and soil returned by Apollo. Furthermore, the detailed analysis of the lunar rocks by many different scientists around the world shows no evidence of their having been on Earth prior to their return.

For every point raised by the conspiracy theorists there seems to be a rational scientific explanation. So is there any likelihood that America faked the moon landings? Not really. As scientists have pointed out, given the amount of work it would have taken to fool the world on such an epic scale it would have been easier to just go to the moon.

IS THERE LIFE ON MARS?

For many years, scientists have speculated about the existence of life on Mars, the Red Planet. In many ways, the planet is similar to Earth, having a cycle of days and nights that corresponds to our own, and also having seasons (although the seasons are different because Mars has a longer year). Since the seventeenth century, our knowledge about the planet, some of it conflicting, has accumulated, so that today many believe that simple life forms – or the potential for them – exist, or have existed, there.

One of the major controversies has centred around whether or not Mars has the basic features necessary to support life as we know it: in particular, water. Most recently, in 2005, the European Space Agency's probe, Mars Express, brought back high resolution photographs of a frozen lake that nestled within a crater in Vastitas Borealis, a great plain in the

BELOW: THE FACE ON MARS: COULD THIS REALLY BE THE FALLEN HEAD OF SOME GARGANTUAN MARTIAN STATUE, AS CLAIMED BY SOME, MOST NOTABLY RICHARD HOAGLAND?

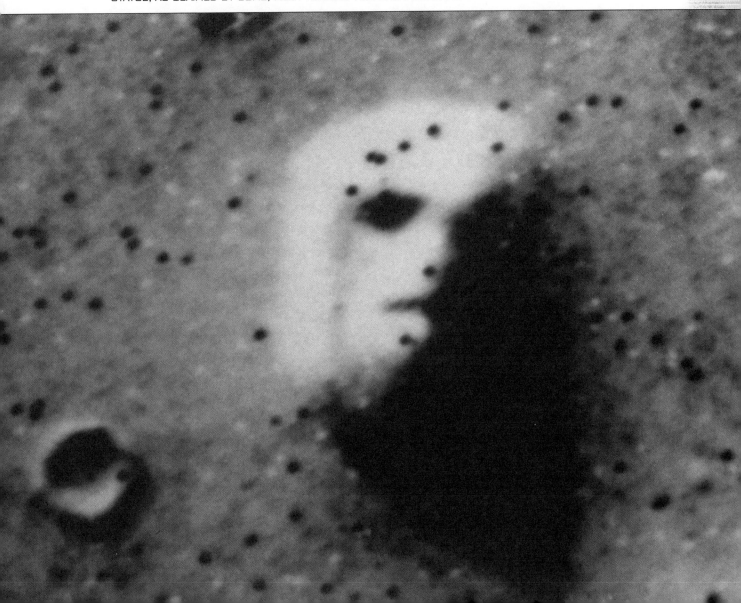

northern part of Mars. The Agency team also discovered a subterranean "frozen sea" on the planet, as well as ice at each of its poles. These finds have prompted the renewed speculation that Mars once supported life and possibly continues to do so.

A PAST CIVILIZATION?

In the late eighteenth century, the scientist William Herschel first demonstrated that the polar ice caps of Mars waxed and waned according to the seasons. A century later, many more features of the planet had been discovered, revealing its similarity to Earth. It appeared to have sea and land masses and it revolved around the sun on a similar axis to the Earth. Then came the extraordinary claim that a telescope sighting had revealed a system of canals on the planet. The claim was later found to be false, but fascination with the idea of life on Mars persisted.

In the nineteenth century, the eminent British scientist William Whewell and the American astronomer Percival Lowell popularized the idea that there was life on Mars. Their ideas inspired H.G. Wells to write his science fiction classic *The War of The Worlds* in 1897. This work of fiction, perhaps more than any other, crystallized our beliefs and fears about life on the

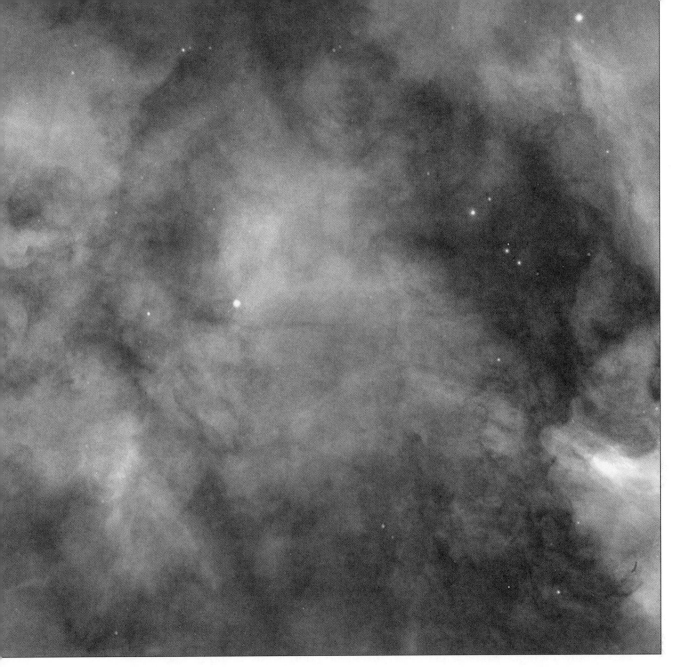

ABOVE: FLIPPING THE BIRD: ALTHOUGH THE KEYHOLE NEBULA MAY APPEAR TO BE GESTURING RUDELY AT THE UNIVERSE, IT IS IN FACT A RANDOM ACCRETION OF COSMIC DUST. THE PHENOMENON OF READING MEANING INTO RANDOM SHAPES OR PATTERNS IS KNOWN AS PAREIDOLIA.

planet. It told the story of alien beings trying to escape from a doomed civilization there by attempting to take over the Earth.

Fact or fantasy?

In the centuries that followed, speculation about an alien civilization on Mars continued, but scientific research seemed to fly in the face of those who believed that there was any type of life at all on Mars. During the 1960s and 1970s, space probes such as Mariner 4 and Viking were sent to make tests, but they appeared to reveal that the planet was a dry, dusty place full of UV radiation, with no sign of rivers or seas. It was hard to believe that any form of life could survive in such a climate. There were one or two dissenting voices who interpreted the findings differently, such as Dr Gilbert Levin, who had designed one of the tests, but most self-respecting scientists gave up the quest to find life on Mars and left speculation to the science fiction enthusiasts.

Then, in 1996, news came that a meteorite from Mars had been found. After an asteroid collision, the meteorite had fallen off Mars and hurtled through space for millions of years, entering the Earth's atmosphere about 13,000 years ago and landing in Antarctica, where it was discovered by a NASA team in 1984. ALH84001, as the lump of rock was called, was examined microscopically by scientists from NASA and Stanford University and was thought to show evidence of fossilized microbes.

At a press conference on 7 August 1996, pictures of the meteorite were shown. Long, worm-like structures, thought to be very tiny bacteria, could be discerned within the rock. This was a stunning discovery and it rekindled interest in the issue of life on the planet Mars once more. Some scientists claimed that the rock had simply undergone chemical changes during its passage to Earth, which had made these long, worm-like patterns on it, but others were convinced that the meteorite had once and for all confirmed that primitive forms of life inhabited the planet, or at least had done so at an earlier date.

THE ORIGIN OF LIFE

In the new millennium, many more discoveries about Mars have been made by NASA. Evidence of subterranean lakes has been found and scientists now believe that Mars was once a planet with seas, which could conceivably have supported forms of life. The gas methane has also been noted to be present in the atmosphere of Mars, a finding that also points to unusual life forms there: organisms that can metabolize carbon dioxide and hydrogen to make methane. A recent survey conducted at a conference of the European Space Agency found that seventy-five per cent of scientists now accept that life on Mars once existed and twenty-five per cent believe that it continues to do so.

Perhaps one of the most exciting aspects of the current climate of research is that it raises questions about how all life begins, not only on Mars but on Earth as well. Today, many scientists believe that there is no real mystery about the origin of life. It is not the hand of God or chance that causes it to begin, but the presence of just the right conditions, such as water and various gases. If the right conditions exist, life springs into being by itself.

The logical conclusion of this theory is that any planet in the universe that has the right conditions, for example water, can support primitive forms of life. It is now thought that there is not only water in the subterranean lakes on Mars, but also on Jupiter's moons, Callisto and Europa. Although it seems unlikely that there are alien beings on Mars – descendants of a vanished civilization who want to take over the planet Earth – a new possibility has been raised, that the universe is teeming with life forms that we have never encountered and as yet, have no knowledge of. And that, perhaps, is an even more fascinating possibility.

THE HOLLOW EARTH

From the earliest times, theories about life under the Earth have abounded. In Ancient Greece, an underworld peopled by the dead was envisaged, which was known as Hades, while Christian mythology conceived of a fiery subterranean place where the damned were sent to endure eternal torture. We know it as Hell. Different versions of these beliefs feature in many ancient religions the world over. But in modern times, there have also been many eminent thinkers and scientists, as well as fiction writers, who have picked up the idea. They describe a "hollow" Earth, often peopled by a prehistoric race, that is reached by a network of subterranean tunnels. Today, few believe that the Earth really is hollow, or that human beings live at the centre of it, but the idea of a different world underground, where some forms of life exist, still excites the imagination. Recent developments in science have shown that such a notion is not merely the stuff of science fiction.

THE IDEA OF A WORLD UNDERGROUND, WHERE LIFE EXISTS, STILL EXCITES THE IMAGINATION.

HALLEY'S INNER SPHERES

In 1692, the renowned English astronomer, Edmund Halley, came up with the idea that the Earth was hollow. As the man responsible for plotting the path of the comet named after him, Halley's opinion was taken seriously. He was an eminent man of science, after all. According to his theory, the reason that the Earth's magnetic field sometimes showed inexplicable variations was because there were other magnetic fields around it, causing opposing gravitational pulls. Halley came up with a new model of the Earth, in which four inner spheres were stacked inside each other. He also advanced the idea that each of these was lit by a luminous gas. The aurora borealis, or Northern Lights, was evidence of this gas, he claimed. This is how the gas looked when it was escaping at the North Pole, where he believed the Earth's crust had thinned. Halley also believed that the spheres could well be inhabited, although he did not specify by what exact forms of life.

Next, a Swiss mathematician named Leonhard Euler proposed that instead of several spheres there was only one, which was at the centre of the Earth. This, he thought, was lit by an inner sun that allowed an advanced civilization to prosper there. Today there is some dispute

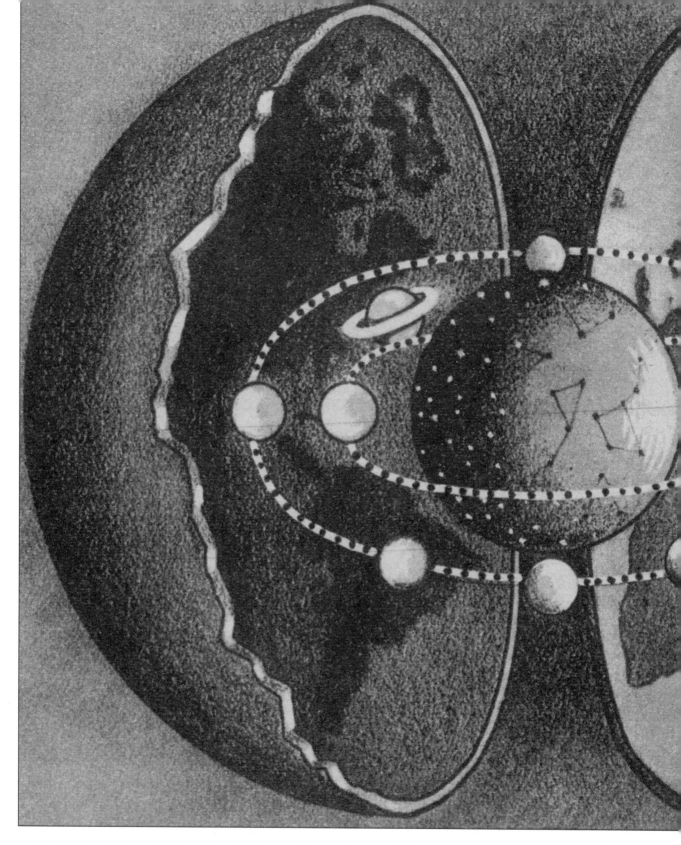

as to whether Euler actually claimed this to be the case, or whether he was merely raising the possibility as a "thought experiment". Whatever the case, his ideas inspired several other thinkers. One of these was another mathematician, a Scotsman called Sir John Leslie, who went on to claim that there were two suns, Proserpine and Pluto, that lit the subterranean realms at the Earth's core.

UNITED STATES EXPEDITION

During the nineteenth century, the idea of a "hollow Earth" became popular among would-be explorers, several of whom suggested making expeditions to find this

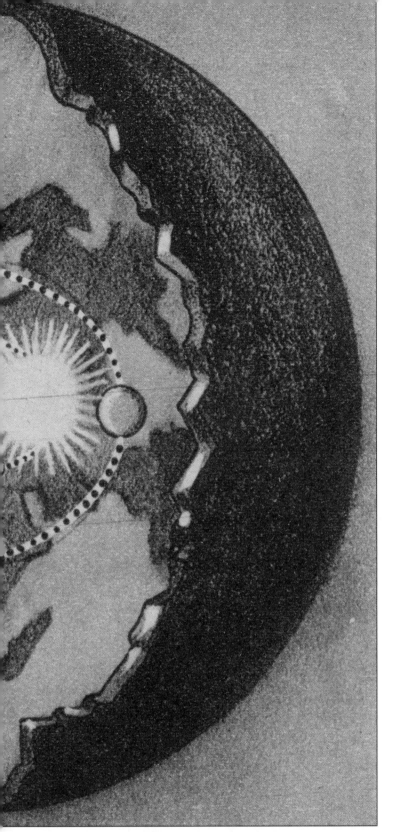

took up the challenge, agitating for the United States government to send out a force, which they did in that year. The Wilkes Expedition, as it was called, did not find the alleged hole, but over a period of years they brought back a great deal of useful information about the continent that came to be called Antarctica.

The next proponent of the hollow Earth theory was William Reed, whose book, *Phantom of the Poles*, was written in 1906. Seven years later, Marshall Gardner wrote *A Journey to the Earth's Interior*, and also made a working model of the Earth's core as he envisaged it. When an extinct species of woolly mammoth was found frozen in the ice in Siberia, Gardner advanced the idea that it had strayed out of the inner zone by passing through the hole at the Earth's pole. According to him, all manner of extinct animals wandered about this subterranean world and here was the evidence for it.

Since that time, new generations of writers have come up with the idea of life in this "hollow Earth": from prehistoric animals to a race of enlightened human beings. It has also been claimed that entrance can be gained to this subterranean civilization through holes in the Earth – in Antarctica, Tibet, Peru and the United States. Not only this, but some believe that UFOs and other extra-terrestrial phenomena emanate from this underworld.

lost world. In 1818, John Cleves Symmes, a businessman, began to raise money to support an expedition to the "hole" at the North Pole where he believed that the inner spheres of the Earth could be entered. He died before the expedition could take place but, in 1838, a newspaperman called Jeremiah Reynolds

WHO KNOWS WHAT AWAITS US AS WE JOURNEY TO THE CENTRE OF THE EARTH, A JOURNEY WE HAVE BARELY EVEN BEGUN?

THE CULT OF KORESH

One of the most notorious "hollow Earth" theorists was Cyrus Read Teed, who took the theory one step further by claiming that the Earth was a completely hollow sphere, with a great human civilization living inside it. He founded a cult in Florida and declared himself to be Koresh, a Messiah, before he died in 1908. Outlandish as his ideas sounded, some aspects of physics and mathematics could be employed to support them and a few scientists continued to investigate his ideas after his death.

By the end of the nineteenth century, and well into the twentieth, claims about the existence of a highly developed, ancient civilization under the Earth's crust continued to abound. Not surprisingly, the idea of a master race proved especially popular among Nazi sympathizers. There was even a theory that Adolf Hitler had escaped to join them – via Antarctica in spacecraft – after his defeat in the Second World War and was still alive many years later.

JOURNEY TO THE CENTRE OF THE EARTH?

Ironically, one of the most persuasive versions of the "hollow Earth" theory came not from a scientist but from an adventure writer: Jules Verne. In his famous book *Journey to the Centre of the Earth*, published in 1864, Verne described a network of tunnels that led from the Earth's surface to underground caves where prehistoric beings live in an underground sea. For many years, scientists thought that such an idea was ridiculous and that nothing could live that far underground, away from the sun. However, recent research has shown that, in fact, there are underground passages leading far into the Earth and that more forms of life flourish there than was previously thought possible. For example, rock-eating bacteria and various kinds of insects such as millipedes and scorpions have been found in places over a mile below ground. No prehistoric creatures such as plesiosaurs have been sighted as yet and there has definitely been no sign of a master race of highly evolved human beings. However, after discovering these simple forms of life deep under the Earth's crust, who knows for certain what else awaits us as science progresses and we journey further into the centre of the Earth?

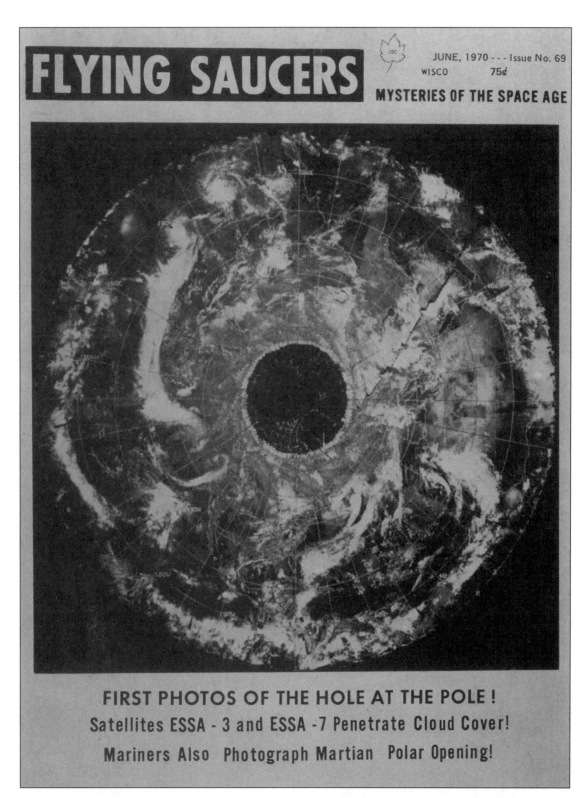

ABOVE: AN EXTREMELY CRUDELY DOCTORED SATELLITE PHOTOGRAPH OF THE EARTH, CLAIMING TO SHOW THE 'HOLE AT THE POLE'. THE FACT THAT BOTH POLES HAVE BEEN VISITED ON SEVERAL OCCASIONS DOES NOT APPEAR TO DISMAY PROPONENTS OF THE HOLLOW EARTH THEORY AT ALL.

CHAPTER FOUR:

THE CHAOS AND CONFUSION OF WAR INEVITABLY
PRODUCES WHOLE RAFTS OF CONSPIRACY THEORIES,
OFTEN FOR THE EXCELLENT REASON THAT THERE ARE,

WAR STORIES

ON ALL SIDES. THE DIFFICULTY LIES IN DISTINGUISHING
THE GENUINE CONSPIRACIES FROM THE 'BLACK'
PROPAGANDA PUT ABOUT BY INTELLIGENCE AGENCIES AS
THEIR CONTRIBUTION TO THE WAR EFFORT.

ADOLF HITLER: DID HE ESCAPE?

The standard account of Adolf Hitler's death is that on 30 April 1945 he committed suicide in his Berlin bunker, shooting himself in the head and possibly also taking a capsule of cyanide. With him was Eva Braun, the mistress he had married on the previous day. After their deaths, both bodies were taken into the garden outside by their few remaining friends, doused with petrol, burned and buried in shallow graves. The bodies were later identified by Soviet forces and a hasty autopsy was performed on the remains.

Today, there are those who continue to question this account. Why were the bodies disposed of in this way? Could it

be, perhaps, that there were in fact no bodies, and that Hitler and Eva Braun had escaped from the bunker to carry on the Nazi campaign from a secret hide-out? If so, where did they go? Was it to the Bavarian Alps, to South America, or even to New Swabia in the Antarctic?

At the time, several important figures, including Joseph Stalin, believed that Hitler had escaped the bunker and was still alive and active somewhere in the world. As the years went by, the conspiracy theories became more bizarre as links were made with Nazi mythologies about the Aryan race. Some suggested that Hitler had disappeared into the hollow earth, or had travelled with aliens to the

LEFT: ADOLF HITLER AT THE *WOLFSSCHANZE*, THE WOLF'S LAIR, HIS HEADQUARTERS IN EAST PRUSSIA, WITH HIGH-RANKING OFFICERS, INCLUDING HERMANN GOERING (3RD LEFT).

star Aldebaran, from where he continues to conduct a campaign to take over the planet Earth.

Far-fetched as some of these theories might be, it is not surprising that there has been a good deal of speculation about the issue. The fact that Hitler's body was so hastily disposed of by the Soviet authorities, and that a satisfactory autopsy was never performed, has meant that we will probably never know the exact circumstances of the death of one of the most notorious leaders in history.

THE FINAL SOLUTION

In the months leading up to the fall of the Third Reich, Hitler, Eva Braun and his top officials retreated to the so-called "Führerbunker" in Berlin to await their final

defeat. By the time the Soviet forces had reached Berlin, Hitler was preparing to commit suicide. He first married his long-term mistress Eva Braun in what must have been one of the most dismal wedding ceremonies ever to take place, using a small map room in the bunker to do so. He then made a will. On the next day, he and his wife said goodbye to their friends and staff, who included Martin Bormann and the Goebbels family. The couple then retreated to Hitler's study, where Bormann and Hitler's valet Heinz Linge later found them lying dead on the sofa. According to their testimony, Hitler was wounded in the head and a pistol lay on the floor. Braun showed no signs of having been shot and was assumed to have taken cyanide.

Linge then told of how he and others on Hitler's staff, including SS guards, took the bodies out to a nearby garden, poured petrol over them, burned them and tried to bury them. However, they could not complete the burial because the Soviet forces were encroaching.

FALSE AUTOPSY

The remains of the bodies were found by Soviet troops from a unit known as the "79th Smersh". The unit, under a forensic pathologist, conducted an autopsy, hoping to discover the cause of death. In order to do so, they used dental records from Hitler's dentist Hugo Blaschke. The

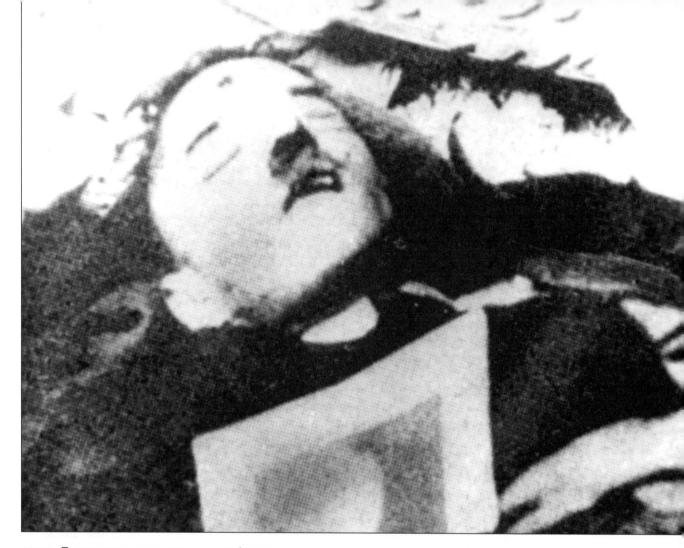

ABOVE: PHOTOGRAPH REPUTED TO SHOW ADOLF
HITLER'S CORPSE IN HIS RUINED UNDERGROUND
BUNKER. THE PICTURE IS CLAIMED TO HAVE BEEN
TAKEN BY A CLOSE MEMBER OF HITLER'S STAFF
WHO WAS IN THE BUNKER WHEN HE SHOT HIMSELF.

pathologist found traces of cyanide in
both bodies and pronounced that Hitler
and his wife had died of cyanide
poisoning. The results were made public
on 16 May 1945.

However, Hitler's staff continued to
attest that the Führer had shot himself, a
death that perhaps seemed more dignified
to them than self-poisoning. Their claims
could not be ignored and the Soviet
authorities finally had to accept that the
autopsy had been wrong. Embarrassed by
the incompetence of the Soviet army over
such an important matter, Stalin issued an
extraordinary statement on 9 June 1945,
to the effect that the remains of Hitler's
body had not been found and that he had
probably escaped.

WHERE DID HE GO?

Stalin and the Soviets made a number of
conflicting statements over the question of
Hitler's body, so that in the end none of
their accounts could be believed. At
different times, for example, they alleged
that Hitler had escaped; that he was being
held alive in prison in the Soviet Union;
and that they had possession of Hitler's
corpse. Not surprisingly, rumours began to
abound and sightings of Hitler began to
be reported. He was thought, for a time, to
be hiding in a secret Nazi stronghold deep
in the Bavarian Alps, along with Martin
Bormann, Artur Axmann (the head of the
Hitler Youth) and Ludwig Stumpfegger
(Hitler's doctor). However, when Axmann
was captured, he maintained that Hitler
had shot himself, while it appeared that
Bormann and Stumpfegger had been shot
by troops while attempting to break out of
Berlin as the Russians closed in.

In the years after World War Two, it was believed that an organization of former SS men, ODESSA, masterminded the operation to help fugitive ex-Nazis settle in other countries, especially South America. There were those who believed that Hitler was hiding in Argentina and others who thought that he was holed up in Spain. There was even a theory that he was living in a moated castle in Westphalia.

HITLER RETURNS?

Harder to credit were the theories that Hitler had travelled to Antarctica and had resumed his earlier career as an artist. He was purportedly painting the frozen landscapes of his new home while planning his next attempt at world domination. Allied to this theory was the notion that he had descended, through a portal at the Pole, to a hollow earth zone populated by an alien master race who were about to take over the planet. Bizarre as these ideas might seem, they were not new to Nazi ideology and, in fact, attempts had been made to establish bases in Antarctica in the early days of the Third Reich. Heinrich Himmler had also championed the cause of Nazi mythologies of the Aryan race and, during his lifetime, Hitler had been revered by some Nazis as a saviour sent by God.

Of course, after Hitler's death – or disappearance – deification was only a short step away. A cult known as "esoteric Hitlerism" grew up: in India, where Savitri Devi and Subhas Chandra Bose claimed that Hitler was a follower of the God Vishnu, sent to restore the Aryans to their former glory; and in South America, where Miguel Serrano put forward the theory that Hitler was planning an imminent return. According to Serrano, Hitler was hiding in Shambhala, a subterranean headquarters in Antarctica, with a master race called the Hyperborean gods. He would eventually emerge to fight the Jews once more and institute a Fourth Reich.

THE REALITY

Today, all that remains of Hitler's body is a skull fragment with a bullet hole in it that was found at the Führerbunker and a section of his jaw that was used for dental identification in the autopsy. Rumour has it that Stalin once owned the skull fragment and used it as an ashtray, in a gesture of ultimate triumph over his former enemy. However, it is now in the Moscow Archives.

But the doubts still linger on. Why do the Russian authorities repeatedly refuse to perform DNA tests on the fragments? Why did they secretly dispose of the rest of Hitler's remains? In modern times, few believe that Hitler is currently hiding underground waiting to unleash Nazi terror on the world once again – he would be over a hundred and fifteen if he were! – but a question still hangs over the exact circumstances of his death. It is certainly possible that we do not know the full story of what happened, even to this day. While that remains the case, conspiracy theories about the death of Adolf Hitler will continue to proliferate.

THE HOLOCAUST

Most people believe that six million Jews in Germany had been rounded up by the end of the Second World War. In what was one of the worst incidents of genocide in human history, they had been gassed, tortured or starved to death in concentration camps. However, there is also a minority view that the Holocaust – the name by which this instance of genocide is known – simply never happened: that it was a gigantic hoax. Adherents of this view claim that the story of the Holocaust is just propaganda. Its aim, they say, was to make American and European non-Jews sympathetic to the cause of the Jewish people by showing them as victims of persecution. Furthermore, the story was fabricated so that the Jews could secure a homeland for themselves at the end of the war, without too much opposition.

On the face of it, such an outright denial of the facts of history seems absurd, but a number of maverick intellectuals and historians have espoused this view, to a greater or lesser extent. They have been accused of anti-Semitism and, indeed, their opinions do seem to be part of a current of extreme anti-Jewish ideology that goes back hundreds of years in Western culture. However, instead of simply dismissing the claims of the "Holocaust deniers" as the ravings of

right-wing ideologues, a number of academics, journalists and committed individuals have decided to look into their theories in detail and refute them by means of a careful historical examination of the facts.

MASS MURDER?

The view of most historians today is that the Nazi government in Germany intentionally persecuted Jews during World War Two and that their eventual aim, as a matter of state policy, was to exterminate them all. To do this, they set

RIGHT: RUSSIAN PHOTOGRAPH OF SOME OF THE SURVIVORS OF AUSCHWITZ, TAKEN AT THE DEATH CAMP'S LIBERATION ON 27 JANUARY, 1945.

up concentration camps, which used a number of methods, including gas chambers, to effect mass murder.

Those who question this view are generally known as Holocaust deniers, although they refer to themselves as "Holocaust revisionists". These groups claim that it was never Nazi policy to exterminate the Jews and that although some Jews were murdered during the war, this was not state policy. They also contend that no gas chambers existed, even at Auschwitz: yet most historians believe that over a million Jews met their deaths in this camp. The "revisionists" typically put the death toll of the Jews who died during World War Two at less than a million or, at most, a million and a half.

THE CONSPIRACY

The view of Holocaust deniers is that the photographs and the film footage of concentration camps that were shown after the war were in fact manufactured by the British and American Allies. (Instead of being the inmates of concentration camps, they claim, the people shown were either German civilians being treated for injuries after Allied bombing incidents or victims of starvation and typhoid.) The Nazis, according to the deniers, did not use gas

chambers to kill their victims. Instead, they claim, the chambers were used to fumigate people en masse, in order to get rid of lice. They admit that many Jews were mistreated during the war but they contend that the top Nazi officials, from Hitler downwards, did not issue orders to exterminate them. Moreover, they go on, most of the Jews in Germany were not murdered: they escaped instead to other countries such as Britain, the United States, Russia and Palestine.

According to the Holocaust deniers, what actually happened at the end of World War Two was that the Jews hatched a plot to demonize the Germans. In this they were supported by the British and American Allies. The purpose of all this was to ensure that Jewish claims to Israel, their potential homeland, would be treated more sympathetically. It has also been alleged that the Soviets also had reason to demonize the Germans. Their object, it has been said, was to make nearby nations such as Poland and Czechoslovakia accept communist rule more easily.

DENIAL OF HISTORY

The Nazis themselves destroyed a great deal of evidence that would have revealed exactly what went on in the concentration camps and it is now clear that, after the war, many of their sympathizers went on to rewrite history. Historians such as the German Friedrich Meinecke and the American Frances Yockey published works with an anti-Semitic bias, followed by less obviously anti-Semitic historians such as Harry Elmer Barnes and James J. Martin. Curiously, Barnes and Martin were both anti-war writers who nevertheless became obsessed with the idea that Germany had been vilified by the British in order to involve the United States in World War Two. In France, Paul Rassinier challenged the received view of the Holocaust. Although he had been held in a concentration camp during the war, because of his socialist affiliations, he was still well known as an anti-Semite.

One of the earliest Holocaust deniers in the United States was Austin App, who published a work called *The Six Million Swindle*. In it, he claimed that the Jews had accused the Germans of mass murder in order to gain large sums of money from the Allies as reparation after the war. Critics countered this claim by pointing out that reparations were actually paid out to survivors, rather than those who had died, primarily for resettlement costs.

By the 1970s, the Holocaust denial movement was in full swing, with the publication of books by Arthur Butz and David Irving, which both claimed that the Holocaust was a fabrication. In 1979, Willis Carto founded the "Institute for Historical Review". Carto was a neo-Nazi, but he also promoted writings by authors from other backgrounds in order to show that the Holocaust deniers enjoyed a wide range of academic support. In 1987, the "Committee for Open Debate on the Holocaust" was set up. This was an anti-

ABOVE: DAVID IRVING, WHOSE LIBEL ACTION
AGAINST DEBORAH LIPSTADT AND PENGUIN
BOOKS FAILED IN 2001.

Semitic organization that conducted an advertising campaign which promoted Holocaust denial.

HATE CAMPAIGNS

In recent years, there have been a variety of responses to the Holocaust deniers, ranging from legal prohibitions (in some European countries, including France and Germany, Holocaust denial is now illegal) to the in-depth analysis of the deniers' claims. In Canada, campaigner Ken McVay set up a newsgroup called alt.revisionism, where he tried to set the Holocaust record straight by providing factual information. He also attempted to report on the nefarious activities of certain Holocaust deniers through his Nizkor Project. This soon incurred their wrath and he received several death threats.

In Britain, Penguin Books published *Denying the Holocaust*, an important rebuttal of David Irving's claims. Written by American author Deborah Lipstadt, the book accused Irving of falsifying evidence to support his case and it further suggested that his motive was essentially anti-Semitic. Irving responded by bringing a libel action against Lipstadt and Penguin. At the end of a complicated trial, during which Cambridge historian Richard J. Evans was hired to examine Irving's work in depth, the judge eventually found in favour of Lipstadt.

Today, the debate over Holocaust denial still rages. On the one hand, there are those who feel that free speech is paramount and that no matter what the Holocaust deniers allege they should be allowed to make their point. On the other hand, many Jews are incensed by the Holocaust deniers: they see their claims as outright anti-Semitism of the worst kind and an incitement to racial hatred. Holocaust denial literature is now openly distributed in some Arab countries, which is something that many critics see as a worrying development. Whatever means are adopted to deal with the problem, it seems clear that denial of the Holocaust is just one of a number of anti-Semitic conspiracy theories that, on close examination, have very little substance.

SINKING OF THE *LUSITANIA*

There are two famous maritime disasters involving great passenger liners during the early part of the last century. One was the *Titanic* and the other the *Lusitania*. The more famous of these is, of course, the *Titanic*, whose sinking was a disaster caused by the emphatic collision of nature and human incompetence. It was so clearly an accident that no conspiracy theorist has yet stepped forward to claim that the iceberg was actually a remote-controlled fake, operated by aliens or Russians.

The sinking of the *Lusitania* in the midst of World War One, on the other hand, has attracted a whole range of conspiracy theories. At the time, it appeared to be a straightforward military matter – a dastardly act of war in which an innocent passenger liner was torpedoed by a German submarine. Over time, however, more and more conspiracy theorists, including many legitimate military historians, have come to suspect that the sinking was a set-up, that the Germans were deliberately encouraged to sink the passenger liner by the British in the hope that the negative publicity would encourage the Americans to join in the war on the British side.

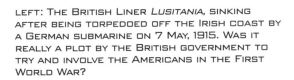

LEFT: THE BRITISH LINER *LUSITANIA*, SINKING AFTER BEING TORPEDOED OFF THE IRISH COAST BY A GERMAN SUBMARINE ON 7 MAY, 1915. WAS IT REALLY A PLOT BY THE BRITISH GOVERNMENT TO TRY AND INVOLVE THE AMERICANS IN THE FIRST WORLD WAR?

This has been an enormously influential conspiracy theory, with its implication that a state might sacrifice the innocent in pursuit of a greater military and political objective. In the years since the event, innumerable other conspiracy theories have grown up around the *Lusitania* example. They range from Pearl Harbor (was the Japanese invasion deliberately encouraged in order to persuade the American people to join World War Two?) to the UK's Birmingham pub bombings (were they actually the work of the security services, designed to promote an anti-IRA backlash?) to the Kuwait invasion (were the Iraqis encouraged to invade in order to spark off the first Gulf War?).

Sunk in eighteen minutes

To return to the case that started all the speculation, was the sinking of the *Lusitania* really the result of a conspiracy by the British or just a regrettable casualty of a terrible war? Let us start by examining the facts. On 1 May 1915 the British passenger liner *Lusitania*, under the command of a Captain Turner, set sail from New York on its journey to the port of Liverpool. On 7 May, when heading past the southern coast of Ireland, the ship crossed paths with a German U-boat. At around 2.10 p.m., and without any warning, the U-boat fired a single torpedo at the *Lusitania*. This caused substantial

initial damage which was then amplified by a second explosion that came from within the ship. The *Lusitania* tilted over onto its starboard side and within eighteen minutes it had sunk.

There was terrible loss of life. As the ship was over on its side the lifeboats from the starboard side could not be used. It was two hours before any other ships were able to respond to the *Lusitania*'s distress signals. The captain of the closest ship, a battle cruiser called the *Juno*, was afraid to approach because of the danger of coming under attack from the U-boat as well. As a result 1,201 people died: nearly two thirds of the ship's 2,000 passengers. Of these, 128 were American citizens.

There was immediate controversy over the acceptability of firing on a passenger liner. Fierce anti-German riots took place in many countries, as people were horrified to learn that the passenger ship had been sunk without warning. The United States in particular was highly critical of the act. The Germans attempted to defend their action, pointing out that they had issued a warning to say that they would attack any British ship as a response to Britain's naval blockade of Germany, which was starving the German people. Nevertheless the catastrophic loss of life that accompanied the sinking of the *Lusitania* made for valuable anti-German propaganda.

Following the sinking, the United States President, Woodrow Wilson, wrote to the German government demanding "reparation so far as reparation was possible". After he had repeated the demand four times, Germany gave in.

They accepted responsibility and agreed to stop sinking passenger ships without warning. This was enough to prevent

ABOVE: *TAKE UP THE SWORD OF JUSTICE* POSTER BY BERNARD PARTRIDGE, URGING AMERICANS TO AVENGE THE SINKING OF THE *LUSITANIA*.

America from becoming immediately involved in the war, but it placed a severe strain on US-German relations. When Germany changed its mind, therefore, and resumed unrestricted submarine warfare in 1917, it was almost inevitable that the United States would enter the war on the side of the Allies.

"AT THEIR OWN RISK"

Gradually, however, historians came to be suspicious of the politically convenient sinking of the *Lusitania* and began to investigate the precise circumstances of its sinking. In his book *The Lusitania*, written in 1972, Colin Simpson, a British journalist, brought these suspicions together. Firstly, he pointed out that despite increased warnings the Admiralty did not assign any escort ships to the *Lusitania*, nor was the *Lusitania* warned that there had been previous U-boat attacks in the area just days before. Secondly, the *Lusitania* appeared to make no effort to avoid attack. It was travelling slowly through a submarine war zone in an area where U-boats were known to lie in wait. Keeping close to the mainland, it failed to use a zigzagging manoeuvre that would make it a harder target to hit.

The first point, in particular, seems telling. The Germans' intentions were far from mysterious. Indeed, on the day the *Lusitania* left New York the German Embassy had placed an advertisement in the American press warning: "that any travelers sailing in the war zone on ships of Great Britain or her allies do so at their

own risk".

So why did the *Lusitania* apparently ignore the warnings and appear to offer itself up like a lamb to the slaughter? The official explanation is that warnings were given. U-boats were not meant to attack passenger ships without first warning them and then helping passengers to safety. The official British position puts the blame squarely on the head of the U-Boat commander – Captain Schweiger – who already had a track record of having destroyed neutral, passenger and hospital ships without warning.

CONSPIRACY OR CASUALTY?

From a strictly naval perspective it is hard to conclusively prove the matter either way – apart from speculating about whether or not any captain would knowingly allow a ship under his command to be blown up while at sea. As for the supporting evidence that Simpson offers, which centres around a meeting at the Admiralty where the sinking of the *Lusitania* was plotted, it seems profoundly dubious. The meeting was allegedly witnessed by one Lieutenant Commander Kenworthy but the fact is that he was not actually at the meeting in question.

So conspiracy or casualty of war? It seems more likely that it was the latter. However, it is not unreasonable to suspect that the impact of the sinking of the *Lusitania*, and the subsequent controversy, may have given other military and political plotters the idea that something similar might just work…

THE BOMBING OF PEARL HARBOR

One of the most damaging military attacks in history was the bombing of Pearl Harbor on the morning of 7 December 1941. On that day, Japanese planes flew over the United States air bases on the island of Hawaii and bombed them all, including the ships anchored at Pearl Harbor. The greatest tragedy was the sinking of the battleship USS *Arizona*, which blew up and sank with over 1,000 sailors aboard. Nineteen other ships were destroyed, as well as many aircraft, and more than 2,000 military personnel were killed that day.

Questions began to be asked in the aftermath of the attack. Why were the intelligence systems of the United States military – one of the most powerful forces in the world – unable to predict such a devastating attack from one of the world's less developed countries. (Japan at the time, of course, was not the technologically advanced society that it is today.) And why did Adolf Hitler declare war on America immediately after the event? Could the attack have been allowed to happen in order to help the American government persuade its people to enter the Second World War? Or is such a betrayal unthinkable?

A SET-UP JOB

On the face of it, it did seem odd that the Americans had no idea that the Japanese were about to bomb their fleet. As many people have pointed out, both at the time

and afterwards, US signals intelligence was extremely effective. The Office of Naval Intelligence (ONI) and the Army Signal Intelligence Service (SIS) had broken several key Japanese codes and ciphers, including the "Purple" cipher which was thought to relay top security information. It was well known that the militaristic Japanese government was preparing for a large-scale war in order to establish their dominance in Asia, a move that would involve undermining the American forces in the Pacific. So why weren't the Americans on the alert?

Some suggest that the American government, under President Franklin D. Roosevelt, knew perfectly well that the Japanese were about to strike, and secretly informed the top military officials at Pearl Harbor to stand aside and let their ships go down. They point out that while the attack was always depicted as a complete disaster for the American military, in actual fact the loss to the Navy – apart from the loss of life – was only five ships in total. Some of the ships damaged in the attack were later repaired and became operational once more. Also, the Japanese could well have sent more bombers to take out the large fuel supplies on the island, but for some inexplicable reason they did not. Thus, the suggestion is that the bombing of Pearl Harbor by the Japanese was a set-up job that Roosevelt and his advisers colluded in, so that the outraged American public would bay for war, which they subsequently did.

CHURCHILL TO BLAME

Other conspiracy theorists, who find it hard to believe that the Roosevelt administration could be quite so callous and cynical, particularly in view of the number of casualties sustained, point to Winston Churchill of Britain as a major culprit. They claim that British intelligence knew about the imminent attack and did nothing to inform Roosevelt about it. The British motive, of course, was that they needed help in the war effort to overcome the Nazis, who were allies of Japan under the Axis Alliance (of Germany, Italy and Japan). By turning a blind eye to Japanese plans for the bombing of the American fleet, the British would help draw the United States into the conflict and thereby gain a powerful new ally. Certainly, the result of the attack was to mobilize public opinion against the Japanese so it made America's entry into the Second World War inevitable.

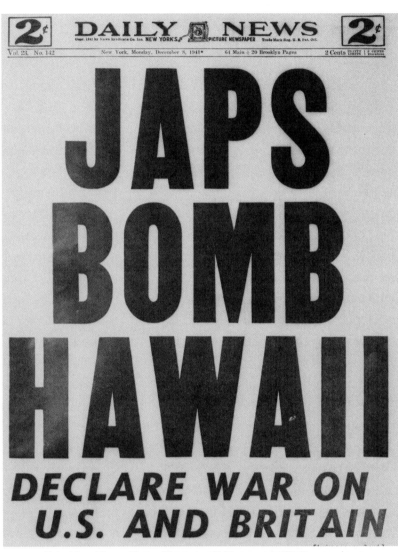

ABOVE: THE NEW YORK *DAILY NEWS* OF 8 DECEMBER 1941 ANNOUNCES THE JAPANESE ATTACKS ON THE AMERICAN BASE AT PEARL HARBOR.

PLOTTERS OR INCOMPETENTS?

Many believe that the bombing of Pearl Harbor was not so much a conspiracy as a series of errors committed by incompetent military officials. Enquiries into what happened have since revealed that general warnings about Japanese aggression were sent to Pacific commands well before the attack, but that the admiral and the general in Hawaii did not take them very seriously. Later, radio warnings were issued as the Japanese force approached Hawaii, but radio contact was temporarily broken. Also, the FBI had assumed that the Navy were tapping the Japanese Consulate but, as it turned out, their bug had been discovered and disconnected. Another factor in the surprise attack was that the US Navy were not familiar with the new technology of torpedo systems. They believed that their ships could not be torpedoed in the shallow water of Pearl Harbor, which was seen as a protection to their fleet. Unbeknown to them, the Japanese had developed torpedoes that operated in shallow water – to devastating effect, as the Americans found out.

A number of individuals have come forward over the years, claiming to have information that shows Pearl Harbor to be a conspiracy. "Seaman Z" claims that he overheard signals from the Japanese, but it has since been counter-claimed that the Japanese did not send any signals at the time because they wished to preserve secrecy as they crept up on the American fleet. In the same way, cryptologists have discussed the so-called "Winds Code" signal, claiming that this Japanese weather report was in fact a signal to the Japanese forces to attack Pearl Harbor. However, to date this seems far from conclusive.

What seems likely is that the British and the American intelligence services were both busy with other issues at the time – Britain, in particular, was in the midst of fighting the Germans in World War Two! Through a series of bungled communications, therefore, they failed to realise the significance of what was going on in the Pacific. There was simply too much conflict taking place in Europe and other parts of the world for America and the Allies to be able to pay much attention to the threat from Japan and deal with it effectively. In addition, various internal rivalries among the top United States military officials in Hawaii at the time prevented efficient intelligence gathering and swift action to avert the attack.

However, many questions still remain unanswered, so much so that conspiracy theories will continue to abound. After all, it is hard to believe that such a devastating strike on Pearl Harbor's "Battleship Row", as it was called, could be the result of sheer incompetence. But, unlikely as it may seem, that might just be the case.

WHAT IS TRUE IS THAT THE BRITISH AND THE AMERICAN INTELLIGENCE SERVICES WERE BOTH BUSY WITH OTHER ISSUES AT THE TIME.

Gulf War Syndrome: Fact or Fiction?

The first Gulf War, prompted by Saddam Hussein's invasion of Kuwait in 1990, has given rise to a whole variety of conspiracy theories. Some suspect that George Bush Senr. deliberately sat by and watched as Iraq invaded Kuwait, happy to use that as an excuse to launch a war that would revive his popularity at home. Others mutter darkly about why the war was called off when Saddam's army was on the run. The question has to be asked: why was the Dictator allowed to lick his wounds and oppress his people for another decade? Perhaps the most enduring and best documented conspiracy theory, however, has to do with the mysterious illness suffered by thousands of combatants, which was known as Gulf War Syndrome.

Gulf War Syndrome began to emerge soon after the end of the war. A steady stream of veterans began to complain of disturbing symptoms. Some were clearly physical while others appeared to be psychological and they included chronic fatigue, loss of muscle control, diarrhoea, migraine, dizziness, memory problems and loss of balance.

As more and more people complained of these symptoms and began talking to each other, members of the Gulf War veterans' groups started to believe that their ailments might have something to do with the war. They began to look for the common causes of their symptoms.

Deadly nerve gas

There were several sinister possibilities – could Saddam Hussein have used biological or chemical weapons after all, or could soldiers have been exposed to unused stocks of the weapons including, perhaps, the nerve gas sarin? Could exposure to the fumes from the oil well fires be responsible? Could it be simply to do with parasites found in the desert? Or local pesticides? One theory that attracted a lot of attention was the possibility that something in the anti-anthrax vaccines the soldiers had been given might be responsible.

Some commentators, however, believed that Gulf War Syndrome was really no more than mass hysteria. In their view, the Gulf War veterans were either suffering from common ailments that were no different to those suffered by the general population, or their complaints were essentially psychosomatic: brought on by all the negative publicity that surrounded the Gulf War. Certain cynics even suggested that in the litigious compensation culture of the United States such complaints were merely a prelude to launching potentially profitable actions for damages.

At first the latter point of view was common but since those days Gulf War

veterans' groups have steadily pressed their case, backed by the findings of various research groups, and popular opinion has gradually begun to shift. A panel chaired by United States Department of Veterans Affairs secretary Anthony Principi reviewed recent studies that suggested that some of the veterans' illnesses were indeed neurological and could be linked to exposure to neurotoxins like the nerve gas sarin, the anti-nerve gas drug pyridostigmine bromide or even certain pesticides. "Research studies conducted since the war have consistently indicated that psychiatric illness, combat experience or other deployment-related stressors do not explain Gulf War veterans illnesses in the large majority of ill veterans," the panel concluded.

If anything, Britain was even more dubious than the United States about the

ABOVE: US MARINES ON FOOT PATROL
THROUGH THE IRAQI DESERT DURING
THE FIRST GULF WAR, 1991.

existence of Gulf War Syndrome, but in recent years the authorities have begun to change their tune. In June 2003 the High Court upheld a claim by a war veteran that the depression, eczema, fatigue, nausea and breathing problems that he had experienced after returning from the Gulf War were directly caused by his military

service. The court's ruling was backed up by a British inquiry in November 2004 which concluded that thousands of British and American Gulf War veterans had been made ill by their service. This report found that war veterans were twice as likely to suffer from ill health than if they had been deployed elsewhere. Rather than fix on one reason, however, the inquiry suggested that their illnesses might be caused by multiple factors including injections of vaccines, the use of organophosphate pesticides to spray tents, low level exposure to nerve gas and the inhalation of depleted uranium dust.

Another British study, which compared 24,000 Gulf War veterans with a control group of 18,000 men, found that those who had taken part in the Gulf war had a lower fertility count. Their partners' failure to conceive was 2.5 per cent vs. 1.7 per cent in the control group and the rate of miscarriage was 3.4 per cent vs. 2.3 per cent. These differences are small but statistically significant.

POISONING OR SHELL SHOCK?

The studies went a long way to winning the argument in the face of those who still maintained that Gulf War Syndrome was essentially stress-related and was similar to "shell shock" after World War I and post-traumatic stress disorder after the Vietnam War. However, as if to prove that there are lies, damn lies and statistics, several other surveys seemed to demonstrate the opposite point of view. A study for the British Ministry of Defence found no correlation between service in the Gulf and death from illness.

Increasingly, many of the veterans' groups began to focus on the question of vaccination. And this is where the conspiracy theories really began to mushroom. Data published in the February 2000 and August 2002 issues of *Experimental and Molecular Pathology* strongly suggested that Gulf War Syndrome was caused by an anti-anthrax vaccine contaminated with squalene. What was worrying about this was that for a long time the United States Army denied that there was any squalene – a substance used in experimental vaccines but not licensed for general use – in the anti-anthrax vaccines. Eventually they were forced to admit that it had been present but claimed that it was because of accidental contamination. Many veterans' groups found this hard to believe, suspecting that United States soldiers had been used as unwitting guinea pigs in a mass trial of an experimental vaccine that was perhaps intended as the model for an anti-HIV vaccine.

The US and UK governments naturally continue to deny that anything of the kind happened. So is Gulf War Syndrome a conspiracy? Or is it just a sad fact of warfare that many combatants end up with stress-related ailments? To date, the jury is still out but it seems likely that the squalene issue may prove to be the key.

LEFT: CARNAGE ON THE BASRA ROAD AS IRAQI TROOPS RETREATED FROM THE ONCOMING ALLIED FORCES AT THE END OF THE FIRST GULF WAR.

CHAPTER FIVE:

OF ALL THE VARIETIES OF CONSPIRACY THEORY WHICH
ABOUND, THE MOST READILY-BELIEVED ARE PERHAPS
THOSE INVOLVING POLITICIANS, WHATEVER THEIR PARTY
ALLEGIANCE. ONE REASON FOR THIS MAY BE THE

POLITICAL COVER-UPS

NUMBER OF POLITICAL COVER-UP THEORIES WHICH HAVE
BEEN DEMONSTRATED TO BE TRUE. THIS SECTION OPENS
WITH THE GRANDADDY OF ALL POLITICAL SCANDALS: THE
WATERGATE AFFAIR.

WATERGATE

The Watergate Affair is one of the key conspiracy tales of our time. Not because it is the most outlandish or extraordinary of conspiracies, but because it turned out to be true. What began as a simple burglary turned out to be a scandal that forced the resignation of a United States president. Here was a real conspiracy and it was uncovered layer by layer until the conspirators – all the way up to President Richard Nixon himself – had to resign or face criminal charges. And perhaps the most lasting effect of the episode was to make sure that conspiracy theorists could no longer simply be written off. Previous events like the assassination of John F. Kennedy now looked more suspicious than ever and the conspiracy theorists, once described as crackpots, were all of a sudden "experts". Never again would the American public simply accept what it was told – even by its president.

The whole extraordinary business began in the early hours of 17 June 1972 at a hotel and office block complex called the Watergate building in Washington, DC. On that day a security guard named Frank Wills noticed a piece of tape being used to hold open a door leading in from the parking garage. Wills removed it, but did not think much of it. He imagined that the cleaning team had perhaps left it there. However, when he returned soon afterwards to discover that someone had put another piece of tape on the door, he decided to call the police. He told them that he suspected that a burglary might be in progress.

The police showed up and at 2.30 a.m. they found five men hiding in an office in the part of the building occupied by the Democratic National Committee. The five men were arrested and were found to include two Cubans, two men with CIA connections and a man named James W. McCord, Jr. who was employed as Chief of Security at a Republican organization called the Committee to Re-elect the President. Alarm bells quickly started to ring. This was clearly no ordinary burglary but a politically motivated one.

Then it emerged that this was not the first Watergate break-in. The same team had already broken into the Democratic Campaign HQ and planted bugs there. Part of the reason for their return was to fix some wiretaps that were not working properly. Further alarm bells went off when the telephone number of one E. Howard Hunt was found in McCord's notebook. Hunt was a former White House consultant and CIA employee.

JUST A THIRD-RATE BURGLARY?
As news of the break-in made its way into the press, questions began to be asked about who in the White House might have known of it. On 19 June The Washington Post reported that a Republican security aide was among the Watergate burglars. The former attorney general John Mitchell, head of the Nixon re-election campaign,

WATERGATE SCANDAL

Kleindienst

Haldeman

Ehrlichman

Magruder

Gray

Dean

denied any link with the operation and the White House did its best to play down the significance of the affair. Nixon press secretary Ron Ziegler called it a "third-rate burglary" and the American public found it hard to accept that a President like Nixon – who was way ahead in all the opinion polls – would sanction a wiretapping operation against his rivals. On 30 August Nixon claimed that White House counsel John Dean had conducted an investigation into the Watergate matter and concluded that no one from the White House was involved. Nevertheless, press speculation refused to go away.

At his 5 September indictment, James McCord identified himself as retired from the Central Intelligence Agency. The Washington, DC district attorney's office began an investigation into the links between McCord and the CIA, and so too did a couple of young journalists from *The Washington Post*, Bob Woodward and Carl Bernstein. They stared to dig deep, aided by leaks from a mysterious anonymous source, known only as "Deep Throat".

During the weeks leading up to the November election The Washington Post ran stories reporting that John Mitchell, while serving as attorney general, controlled a secret Republican fund that was used to finance widespread intelligence-gathering operations against the Democrats. Then it reported that FBI agents knew that the Watergate break-in was part of a massive campaign of political spying and sabotage that was being conducted on behalf of the Nixon re-election effort. Still the public took no notice and Nixon was duly re-elected by a landslide.

On 8 January 1973 the original burglars, along with Hunt and another former intelligence operative turned White House security consultant named Gordon Liddy, went to trial. All except McCord and Liddy pleaded guilty and all were convicted of conspiracy, burglary and wire-tapping. The accused had been paid

to plead guilty but say nothing and their refusal to confess to the crimes angered the trial judge John Sirica (known as "Maximum John" because of his harsh sentencing). Sirica handed down thirty-year sentences, but indicated that he would reconsider if the group would be more co-operative. McCord capitulated and wrote a letter to the judge in which he claimed that the defendants had pleaded guilty under duress. He said they had committed perjury at the urging of John Dean, counsel to the President, and John Mitchell, when he was the attorney general.

SECRET TAPES

By now the "third-rate burglary" had become a major scandal. The revelations just kept coming. On 6 April John Dean, the White House Counsel, began co-operating with the Watergate prosecutors. Nixon promised fresh investigations but began to look like a man engaged in a desperate cover-up. Dean was sacked and other presidential advisers were forced to resign, but the press were still not satisfied. Dean testified that he had mentioned the Watergate break-in to the President thirty-five times. Nixon denied it. But then the existence of tapes that contained all of the President's conversations in the Oval Office was discovered.

Nixon at first refused to release the tapes, but then handed over edited transcripts. Legal moves eventually forced him to hand over the original tapes, but

parts of them were discovered to have been erased. Finally, Congress began to consider an extraordinary move – to impeach the President. At first this seemed impossible but then, with the August 1974 discovery of the "Smoking Gun" tape that proved that Nixon knew of the cover-up operation, the impeachment process looked certain to go ahead. On 8 August Nixon accepted that the game was up and announced his resignation.

And so the most sensational conspiracy case in American history came to its end. Or did it? Today, there are any number of revisionist Watergate theories out there. Some say that the Democrats deliberately set Nixon up. Other suggest that Dean himself was responsible for the whole business and had ordered the break-in to cover up a prostitution scandal in which he was allegedly implicated.

In the final analysis though, it seems that the conspiracy theorists should learn to quit while they are ahead. Watergate was a conspiracy and it went all the way to the top. The guilty parties were even punished for it. What more satisfying end to a major conspiracy could there possibly be?

BELOW: BOB WOODWARD AND CARL BERNSTEIN, THE JOURNALISTS WHO BROKE THE WATERGATE STORY IN THE PRESS.

THE IRAN–CONTRA CONSPIRACY

One of the most notorious conspiracies of the Reagan administration was the Iran–Contra affair, in which the United States government sold arms to Iran (supposedly an enemy state), and also funded anti-Communist forces, known as the Contras, in Nicaragua. Both the Iranian and the Nicaraguan activities were not only against declared United States government policy but were also in contravention of laws passed by Congress. When the activities were exposed, there was a scandal and several important figures were indicted, including Lieutenant-Colonel Oliver North, a key military official and John Poindexter, National Security Adviser under Ronald Reagan. President Reagan himself was forced to make an appearance on television to explain his actions to the American public. He maintained that he considered what he had done to be right and he survived the scandal, but it damaged the reputation of his administration considerably.

DOUBLE DEALING

At the time that the scandal broke, in the mid-1980s, Nicaragua was in the midst of a civil war between the Marxist government, known as the Sandinistas, and their opponents, the anti-Communist Contras, who were engaged in guerrilla warfare. The country's proximity to the

United States meant that they were always vulnerable to influence from their powerful neighbour and it was clear that the United States was opposed to the Marxist government in power there. However, the fact that the United States was funding the Contras, in the hope that they could topple the left-wing government, did not become public knowledge for some time. Even more shocking, it later transpired that the money that was used to fund the Contras had come from the sale of American arms to Iran, which at the time was being run by an Islamic fundamentalist government and was ostensibly an enemy of the United States. What came out was that the Americans were hoping that the sale of arms to Iran would persuade the Iranians to intercede with Islamic terrorists in Lebanon, who were holding hostages there. However, this double dealing was completely against international law and was also hypocritical since, in public, President Reagan was critical of the regime in Iran.

ARMS FOR HOSTAGES

To solve the problem of how to get the hostages back, a secret deal was made in which arms were sold to Iran in exchange for the release of the hostages in Lebanon. The proposal for the plan came from the Israeli government, who suggested that

the United States should broker a deal to sell hundreds of missiles to Iran, which at the time was fighting the Iran–Iraq war. The missiles were designed to defeat armoured tanks and they boasted important new features, including laser range-finders and thermal optics. In

ABOVE: US MARINE COLONEL OLIVER NORTH TESTIFIES DURING THE IRAN-CONTRA CONGRESSIONAL HEARINGS, DURING WHICH HE ADMITTED SELLING ARMS TO IRAN TO FUND NICARAGUAN CONTRAS.

exchange, the terrorists in Lebanon that were holding Benjamin Weir, an American hostage, would release their captive.

The deal took place under the direction of Defense Secretary Caspar Weinberger and the first American hostage was freed in September. Two months later, a similar transaction took place in which 500 Hawk anti-aircraft missiles were to be shipped to Iran. The purpose of the Hawk missiles was to shoot down aircraft and they could be launched from the ground into the air by a single soldier. However, the cost of these missiles was so high that the proposal needed to go through Congress. Robert McFarlane, the President's National Security Adviser, pressed for the deal to go ahead and, in 1985, the first shipment of missiles reached Iran. Negotiations continued into 1986, setting out a new deal in which an intermediary, Manucher Ghorbanifar, would sell arms to Iran in exchange for the hostages.

However, the plan began to founder when, after releasing their hostages, the terrorists began to take new ones. Also, Ghorbanifar and Colonel Oliver North, the aide to Reagan's national security adviser, were accused of selling the weapons at highly inflated prices.

FUNDING THE CONTRAS

It later emerged that the money made from the sale of arms to Iran was being used to fund the Nicaraguan Contras in their bid to oust the democratically elected government there. Earlier in the decade, a scandal had broken when it was discovered that the CIA were secretly providing help to the Contras and legislation, under the Boland Amendment

of 1982, had been drawn up to prevent this happening again. However, National Security Adviser John Poindexter and his aide Oliver North had managed to find a legal loophole. They conducted their business under the auspices of the National Security Council, which was not subject to the Boland Amendment.

It was just a matter of time before the press discovered what was going on and blew the whistle on the scandal. The arms for hostages deal was exposed in 1986, after an incident in which it was discovered that guns were being smuggled into Nicaragua for use by the Contras. Oliver North and Fawn Hall, his secretary, came under scrutiny after they destroyed documents concerning the deal. The administration was eventually forced to admit what had happened.

FINDING THE CULPRITS

In order to allay criticism, President Reagan ordered a commission, later known as the Tower Commission, to look into the problem. He alleged that he had no idea that arms were being exchanged for hostages and that the profits from the arms were being used to support the Contras in Nicaragua. The Commission named North and Poindexter, mentioned that Weinberger was also involved and suggested that the President should have been more aware of the activities of his staff. In 1987, Congress indicted McFarlane, Poindexter and North and they were convicted on several counts, but these convictions were later overturned.

Reagan himself survived the scandal, although it became clear, as information emerged, that he had been involved in the deals, at least to some degree.

The Iran–Contra conspiracy remains one of the biggest scandals to emerge under the Reagan administration. It showed how top government officials acted with no regard for Congressional or international law. They made up their own rules in a secret political game, both within and outside America, that flouted the

ABOVE: NICARAGUAN CONTRA GUERILLAS PICTURED IN TRAINING. DURING THE 1980s, WITH US ECONOMIC AND MILITARY SUPPORT, THE CONTRAS WAGED A VICIOUS STRUGGLE AGAINST THE NICARAGUAN SANDINISTA GOVERNMENT.

conventions of democracy and fair play. The fact that all the players in the game were ultimately pardoned has caused many commentators to suggest that conspiracy continues to lie at the heart of the Machiavellian business of government – not just of totalitarian states, but of our great democracies as well.

THE CIA AND SALVATOR ALLENDE

There are many conspiracy theories about the CIA and its involvement in destabilizing left-wing regimes in foreign countries around the world. Some of them are difficult to take seriously and are born of sheer paranoia, while others seem credible but are difficult to prove. However, in the case of the overthrow of Salvator Allende in the Chilean coup of 1973, it is clear that the CIA ran a covert operation over a number of years in order to undermine the popularity of the democratically elected president. It is also apparent that it was involved in the events that led to his downfall.

THE RISE OF ALLENDE
Born in Valparaiso, Chile, in 1903, Salvator Allende studied medicine and became involved in radical politics while still a student. In 1933, he helped set up the Chilean Socialist Party, whose aim was to pursue Marxist policies outside the influence of the Soviet Union. He became Minister of Health in 1939 in the government of Aguirre Cedra before becoming a senator. After that he ran for President, finally achieving office in 1970, after three unsuccessful attempts.

As the new President, Allende pledged to solve Chile's pressing economic and social problems. At the time of his presidency, inflation and unemployment had reached drastic proportions and over half of the country's children were suffering from malnutrition. Allende immediately introduced wage increases, froze prices, nationalized the banking and copper industries and began to institute land reforms. This made him extremely unpopular with the United States, which had wide-ranging corporate interests in Chile.

THE COUP
In September 1970, President Richard Nixon instructed Henry Kissinger, the American Secretary of State, to support a coup against Allende's socialist government in Chile. Kissinger now claims that although he initially followed the President's orders, he and the CIA later ceased to be involved in the plot. Three years later, there actually was a military coup in Chile which removed Allende and his government from power and installed General Augustus Pinochet as president instead. Allende is thought to have committed suicide during the fighting, by shooting himself with a gun given to him by Fidel Castro.

General Pinochet went on to rule Chile as an authoritarian dictator until 1990 and during his regime he became notorious for

RIGHT: THE PROBLEM: SALVADOR ALLENDE WITH CUBAN DICTATOR FIDEL CASTRO. THE CIA FEARED THAT ALLENDE WOULD BUILD CLOSER CONTACTS WITH CASTRO, AMERICA'S PUBLIC ENEMY NUMBER ONE.

ABOVE: THE SOLUTION: A US-BACKED MILITARY COUP IN SANTIAGO, UNDER THE CONTROL OF GENERAL PINOCHET. PINOCHET WOULD BECOME ONE OF THE MOST HATED DICTATORS IN SOUTH AMERICA.

human rights abuses. Kissinger and the CIA were accused of being involved in those abuses during that time. They purportedly assisted in the organization of "Operation Condor", a secret, right-wing military group that kidnapped and murdered hundreds of the regime's political opponents throughout the decade of the 1970s.

CIA INVOLVEMENT?

It has now been proved that from 1963 to 1973 the CIA did its utmost to prevent a socialist government from gaining power in Chile. During the 1964 elections they helped pay expenses for the opposition. They also ran national propaganda campaigns on radio, TV and in the press with the object of demonstrating that Allende's communist policies would ruin the country. Six years later, in the presidential election of 1970, the agency conducted a campaign against Allende himself. Despite this, however, Allende went on to win the election by a narrow margin. After that, the CIA tried to persuade other Chilean politicians to tamper with the political process in order to oust the newly ensconced president,

even to the point of organizing a coup. When that also failed, the United States began to exert economic pressure on the country.

In addition to his enemies in the United States, Allende had plenty of opponents in Chile itself, people who stood to lose wealth and power as a result of his policies. Moreover, the change in the political direction of the country had caused a number of economic and social problems, which were exacerbated by the hostile stance of the United States. In particular there was a strong current of opposition against Allende within the military, and it was from this quarter that the coup of 1973 was mounted against him.

Today, it is still unclear to what degree the CIA were involved in organizing the coup. There is no doubt, however, that some form of covert action took place in Chile during Allende's years in office and that the CIA was still continuing its campaign against him at the time of the coup.

PROJECT FUBELT

Numerous investigations have helped clarify the role of the United States in the Chilean coup, although some believe that the full truth has yet to come out. Former Secretary of State Henry Kissinger has admitted that although Nixon did not have a direct hand in the coup, he "created the conditions as great as possible" for it.

Also, according to recently declassified documents, the United States government tried to oust Allende under "Project Fubelt" in 1970. At that time, the CIA had links with General Roberto Viaux, who was planning a coup against the president which involved kidnapping the army chief of staff General René Schneider. (Schneider opposed the idea of military intervention on constitutional grounds.) The coup misfired in an episode that led to the death of General Schneider.

Afterwards, Kissinger maintained that the CIA had withdrawn from the plot. There is still no hard evidence to connect the CIA with the subsequent coup in 1973, but its involvement in this earlier attempt naturally fuels suspicion. It has also been pointed out that much of the information remains classified. In recent years, it has also become clear that although the United States government publicly criticized Pinochet, the CIA supported the military junta and paid many of the officers to become informants. Some of these officers, it has been alleged, were party to human rights abuses, although the CIA has denied this claim.

AFTERMATH

Victims of the Pinochet regime have now begun to take legal action against the United States government and the CIA. In 2001, the family of General René Schneider accused Kissinger of plotting to murder the general because of his opposition to the military coup. It was discovered that although the CIA had discussed kidnapping Schneider they had not intended to kill him. Kissinger maintained that he and Nixon had decided not to back the coup at the last minute.

Whatever the truth of the matter, it remains clear that over a number of years the role of the CIA in Chile was to undermine the career of Salvador Allende and prevent the success of a socialist government by means of a series of underhand dealings with his opponents. The CIA eventually achieved its aim – but the popular image of the United States as a protector of democracy was compromised. Thus, in the case of Chile, the conspiracy theorists were proved right.

ABOVE: THE PLAYERS: US SECRETARY OF STATE HENRY KISSINGER, AND CHILEAN DICTATOR GENERAL PINOCHET. AS OF 2005, THE CHILEAN COURTS ARE SLOWLY BEGINNING TO CATCH UP WITH PINOCHET.

Marc Dutroux: A Paedophile Conspiracy?

Normally conspiracy theories come from the outside. Sceptical members of the public speculate about the truth behind something they have seen on the news or read about in the newspapers. Occasionally, however, such theories are actively put about by participants in the actual events. There are two possible explanations for such theories. One is that the participants are telling the truth – they know they are just scapegoats that are caught up in a wider conspiracy. The other possibility is that people who are caught red-handed while committing terrible acts will point to a larger conspiracy in the hope that it will get them off the hook.

Mostly it is quite easy to tell the difference, but in the case of the Belgian paedophile and serial murderer Marc Dutroux the uncertainty still lingers on. Did Dutroux murder four little girls purely for his own perverted pleasure, or was he – as he stated in court – merely the instrument of a paedophile conspiracy that reached all the way to the very top of Belgian society.

Let us start by examining the facts of the matter. Marc Dutroux was born in Brussels, Belgium's capital city, on 6 November 1956. He was the eldest of six children born to Victor and Jeanine Dutroux. Both parents were teachers and Dutroux claimed that they frequently beat him. However Dutroux's statements on

this or any other matter have to be regarded with extreme caution because he was an inveterate liar. What we do know is that the couple split up in 1971, when Dutroux was fifteen. Soon afterwards he left home, drifted into petty crime and, according to some press accounts, became a homosexual prostitute.

However, by the time he was twenty he had found a trade as an electrician, and had married his first wife and had two children with her before she divorced him on the grounds of infidelity and violence. One of the women with whom he had extra-marital affairs was Michele Martin who later became his second wife. She also evidently shared his darker sexual predilections.

In 1989 the pair were convicted of child abuse, on the specific charge of jointly abducting five girls for Dutroux to rape. For his part Dutroux was sentenced to thirteen years in prison. However, he was released for good behaviour after serving only three years.

The dungeon
Before going to prison, Dutroux had also become involved in a range of criminal enterprises from mugging to drug dealing. On his release from prison he made no effort to find legal work. Instead, the first thing he did was to build a dungeon underneath a house in the town of

ABOVE: MARC DUTROUX IS ESCORTED FROM HIS HOUSE DURING HIS TRIAL FOR RAPE, KIDNAP AND MURDER, MARCH 2004. DUTROUX WAS CONVICTED OF MURDER AND SENTENCED TO LIFE IMPRISONMENT WITH NO HOPE OF PAROLE.

Charleroi, one of several houses he had bought with his criminal gains. The dungeon was not only going to be used for the abuse of children but also to film that abuse and sell the videos to a network of paedophiles.

As in so many serial killer cases, it is quite possible that Dutroux is guilty of more crimes than we are aware of. It also seems unlikely that his dungeon was unused for three years. However the first definite atrocity we know of began on 24 June 1995 when two 8-year-old girls, Julie Lejeune and Melissa Russo, were abducted from near their homes in Liège, Belgium. They were taken to Dutroux's dungeon where they were kept as sexual playthings, being almost certainly abused by the members of a paedophile ring.

Two months later the girls were still in the dungeon when Dutroux and an accomplice Bernard Weinstein abducted two teenage girls, An Marchal, aged nineteen, and Eefje Lambreks, aged seventeen, from the seaside town of Ostend. They were taken to Weinstein's house to be raped by Dutroux and Weinstein. At some point both girls were killed and then, for unknown reasons, Dutroux also killed Weinstein. He buried all three under a shed in the garden.

FEEDING THE DOGS, NOT THE CHILDREN

Meanwhile the two other girls were still alive in the Charleroi dungeon. The police received a tip-off that Dutroux had captured the girls but during a search of the house they failed to notice the dungeon – even though they had been specifically told of its existence. When in December 1995, Dutroux was sentenced to four months in prison for car theft, he told Michele Martin to feed the two girls. Almost unbelievably she failed to do this. Even though she visited the house regularly to feed Dutroux's dogs she claimed to have been too scared to go down into the cellar and feed the girls. As a result they starved to death.

When Dutroux came out of prison he found the dead bodies, put them in a freezer for a while and then buried them in the garden of another of his houses, in Sars-le-Buissiere. On 28 May he started to restock the dungeon. He kidnapped Sabine Dardenne, aged fourteen, and took her to the dungeon. He told her that he was rescuing her from a paedophile gang who were responsible for kidnapping her and were awaiting a ransom from her family. Nevertheless his "protection" didn't stop him from raping her some twenty times, as she recorded in her diary. After seventy-two days in the dungeon, she was joined by Dutroux's latest victim Laetitia Delhez, aged twelve, on 9 August.

This time, however, a witness had noticed a suspicious car close to where Delhez was abducted. The car belonged to Dutroux and on 13 August the police arrested Dutroux and Martin at the house in Sars-le-Buissiere. Two days later they raided the Charleroi house and this time they found the dungeon and were able to bring out Dardenne and Delhez alive. Over the next few weeks Dutroux began to confess, always insisting that he was merely a pawn in a much wider conspiracy, and he led the police to the bodies of his five victims as the nation looked on in horror.

CORRUPTION IN HIGH PLACES

That horror turned to anger as the prosecution of the case seemed to drag on endlessly, fuelling speculation that it was being deliberately sabotaged by paedophiles in high-ranking jobs. The lead prosecutor was then removed from his job on a flimsy pretext. The Belgian public began to suspect that Dutroux's talk of a conspiracy was not merely an attempt to deflect attention from his own guilt. They mounted a huge demonstration against the corruption of the authorities.

Two years later Dutroux briefly escaped custody, further fuelling the public's anger and forcing the resignation of two government ministers. It was another six years, March 2004, before the case at last came to trial. Dutroux continued to insist that he was just a pawn in a huge conspiracy, but the brave testimony of the surviving victims, particularly the enormously impressive Sabine Dardenne, was devastating. She told the court that Dutroux had told her also that there was a wider conspiracy. He even presented himself as her protector. But then she revealed that she had never seen any of those alleged paedophiles. Instead it was Dutroux, and Dutroux alone, who had raped her repeatedly.

The defence tried to stick to its conspiracy theory. They pointed out that there was DNA from unknown persons in the dungeon. Dutroux tried to portray Nihoul, a con-man and a regular visitor to Belgium's sex clubs, as the lynch-pin of the conspiracy. However, while there was evidence that suggested that rich and powerful men were connected to Nihoul and would attend the same orgies (involving consenting adults), there was no proof that they were involved in Dutroux's much more sinister world.

The judge and jury clearly considered Dardenne's evidence to be the more compelling account. Dutroux was found guilty of murder and sentenced to life in prison without the possibility of parole. Michele Martin was sentenced to thirty years for her unspeakable cruelty in abetting Dutroux and letting the two little girls starve to death. Jean-Michel Nihoul, meanwhile was acquitted of the kidnapping charges that linked him to Dutroux but was sentenced to ten years for smuggling drugs and people.

So were the jury right to reject the notion of a wider conspiracy? It seems likely. The suggestions of a cover-up are probably more to do with a mixture of extraordinary police incompetence and some high level interference relating to involvement in Nihoul's orgies rather than Dutroux's murders. As for the suggestion that there was Satanic abuse, this, like almost all cases of alleged Satanic abuse, seems to be the product of over-active imaginations.

THE TUSKEGEE SYPHILIS EXPERIMENT

The Tuskegee Syphilis Experiment, which was run between 1932 and 1972, was one of the most shocking scientific studies ever to take place. In it, 399 black men, most of whom were poor Alabaman sharecroppers, took part in a supposed treatment for "bad blood" which would cure them of illness. They were never told that their illness was syphilis and that – except at the beginning of the study – they were receiving no treatment at all. What was in fact happening was that doctors were studying the ravages of the untreated disease and waiting for them to die so that they could perform autopsies on the corpses. The supposed aim of the experiment was to find out more about the disease and to determine whether it affected black people differently to whites. However, at the end of the study, which continued over several decades, it was suggested that no important knowledge had been yielded. Meanwhile, many men had met their deaths, after terrible illnesses whose symptoms included paralysis, blindness, heart disease, tumours and insanity. Not only this, many of the men's wives had become infected and their children born with congenital syphilis.

LEFT: BLACK AMERICAN COMBAT AIRMEN, 1942, TRAINED UNDER THE TUSKEGEE AIR PROGRAM. THE TUSKEGEE SYPHILIS EXPERIMENT WAS LESS WELL-PUBLICIZED, HOWEVER.

"SPECIAL FREE TREATMENT"

The study was started at the Tuskegee Institute, under the auspices of the United States Public Health Service. Its initial aim was to study a group of black men with untreated syphilis for a period of months and then treat the disease. However, several of the doctors wanted to continue the programme for a longer period and fearing that the men would not want to co-operate if they knew the truth – that they were being studied to see how long it took them to die of the disease – the doctors began to misrepresent what was going on. They began to write to their "patients" advertising "special free treatment", when all they were doing was performing diagnostic tests. These included painful and dangerous lumbar punctures, from which the patients derived absolutely no medical benefits at all.

SHAMEFUL ETHICS

Penicillin became the standard treatment for syphilis in 1947 and there were government initiatives to treat the population in as rapid a manner as possible. Nationwide campaigns invited citizens to attend treatment centres and men who were called up into the army were screened for the disease and given treatment. The subjects of the Tuskegee Syphilis Experiment, however, were excluded from the programme but they accepted the story that they were being treated already. In this way, syphilitic men were prevented from gaining treatment that would have saved their lives.

It was not until 1966 that the story broke in the national press. Peter Buxtun, who worked for the Public Health Service in San Francisco as a venereal disease investigator, became aware of the experiment and wrote to his superiors to inform them of what was going on. However, he was told that the experiment needed to go ahead and that it would not be curtailed until all the subjects had died and the autopsies had been performed. Frustrated by this brush-off, Buxtun went to the newspapers and in 1972 several national newspapers ran stories on the experiment. The experiment was quickly brought to a halt as a result of the adverse publicity and the surviving subjects and their families compensated and promised free medical treatment in the future.

Two years later, legislation was put into effect to regulate medical experiments involving human beings. However, it was not until 1997 that a public apology was made by the President of the United States. In the presence of the five remaining survivors of the study (only eight were left in total) President Clinton formally apologized for the behaviour of the United States government and called it "shameful".

A CONSPIRACY AGAINST ETHNIC MINORITIES

The fact that the study was conducted on

black people led many to accuse the scientists who mounted it of racism. However, this was complicated by the fact that several of the staff in charge of the experiment were African-Americans. The experiment was also conducted under the auspices of one of America's most respected black universities, the Tuskegee Institute, set up by Booker T. Washington. The hospital of the university loaned medical facilities to the Public Health Service in order that they could conduct the experiment and local African-American doctors also became involved.

One of the central figures in the drama was a black nurse called Eunice Rivers. She had worked with the subjects for nearly forty years and was trusted by most of them. Defending her behaviour, she claimed that she was simply carrying out the orders of the doctors and was not in a position to diagnose the patients' illnesses.

Strangely, both black doctors and nurses felt that they were helping solve the problem of venereal disease in the Afro-American community, and they were deeply committed to health programmes that helped the poorest people in their area, Macon County. It was as if they simply could not see that human beings should not be treated in this way, as just a means to an end, even in the cause of supposedly extending medical knowledge.

Also perplexing is the way in which the study was set up. Once it had been dismantled, many questions were asked. Why, for example, had it been thought

necessary to find out the differences between the progress of the disease on white people and black people? The study was set up to find out whether it was true that black people experienced cardiovascular problems as a result of syphilis infection, whereas white people were more susceptible to neurological malfunctioning. But how this information would have helped treat the disease remains unclear.

Not only that, but the scientific methodology in the study was flawed. The investigation was designed to show how the disease progressed when untreated but the subjects had already been treated – with contemporary treatments such as mercurial ointments – in the first few months of the programme, before it was decided to extend the study. The thinking behind the experiment was so unclear and the scientific gains were so questionable that one can only assume that an extraordinary level of, possibly unconscious, racism must have blinded the scientists to the fact that they were treating their subjects in a completely inhuman way.

In several later sociological studies the Tuskegee syphilis experiment was shown to have had an adverse effect on health programmes directed at African-Americans, who unsurprisingly increasingly mistrusted the public health authorities. The episode caused lasting damage and it is remembered as one of the most appalling conspiracies ever to take place in American history.

CHAPPAQUIDDICK

The three Kennedy brothers dominated the American political landscape during the 1960s and each one of them was involved in a sensational news story that in turn led to a whole range of conspiracy theories. In the case of the two elder brothers, John and Robert, the sensational events were their assassinations. However, their younger brother, Edward "Teddy" Kennedy, hit the headlines because of the death of a young woman named Mary Jo Kopechne.

Mary Jo Kopechne was twenty-eight years old at the time of her death. She had worked in Washington since graduating

BELOW: SENATOR EDWARD KENNEDY (RIGHT) AND HIS BROTHERS, JOHN AND ROBERT, ARE SHOWN AT HYANNISPORT, MASSACHUSETTS.

from college, first as secretary to Senator George Smathers and then to Robert Kennedy. During Kennedy's presidential campaign she had become part of a devoted and hardworking team known as the "boiler room girls". Following Robert Kennedy's assassination in 1968 the "boiler room girls" had been busy closing up his office. As a way of thanking them for their hard work, Robert's brother Edward Kennedy, also a Senator, had invited them to spend a weekend at Martha's Vineyard. They would watch a yachting race at Edgartown on 18 July 1969 and then a party would be held in their honour on Chappaquiddick island.

CRASHED OVER BRIDGE

The party was a small affair. The six "boiler room girls" all attended – Kopechne, Susan Tannenbaum, Maryellen Lyons, Ann Lyons, Rosemary (Cricket) Keough and Esther Newburgh – and the other guests were six men, all of them married but without their wives in attendance. The men were Edward Kennedy, US Attorney Paul Markham, Joe Gargan (Kennedy's cousin and lawyer), Charles Tretter, Raymond La Rosa and John Crimmins. Gargan rented the venue, called Lawrence Cottage, and John Crimmins supplied the alcohol. He brought three half gallons of vodka, four fifths of scotch, two bottles of rum and two cases of beer – an ample amount for twelve people, when at least two of them were not drinking.

According to Kennedy's account, what happened next was that Kennedy offered to drive Kopechne home at around 11.15 p.m., a journey that involved catching the ferry from the island back to Edgartown. Unfortunately, instead of turning left on to the road to the ferry he turned right and found himself on an unfamiliar road that led him unexpectedly to a narrow bridge. The car crashed over the side of the bridge and fell into the water, turning over in the process.

STATE OF SHOCK

At first Kennedy thought he was going to drown but then the door burst open and he was carried to the surface. He looked around for Kopechne but he could not see her. Although he dived down the current was too strong and he was unable to get into the car to save her. Suffering from concussion and shock, he made his way back to the cottage where he enlisted the help of Gargan and Markham. They returned to the car and tried again to dive down, still without success. Still in a state of shock, Kennedy returned to the ferry landing and swam across to the mainland, where he returned to his hotel. It was only in the morning that he came to his senses and called the police to report the accident.

This account was more or less accepted by the police. Kennedy was summoned to court to answer the charge of either failing to remain at the scene of an accident he had caused or at least failing to report it. He was let off with a two months' suspended sentence for this crime, despite the fact that the law

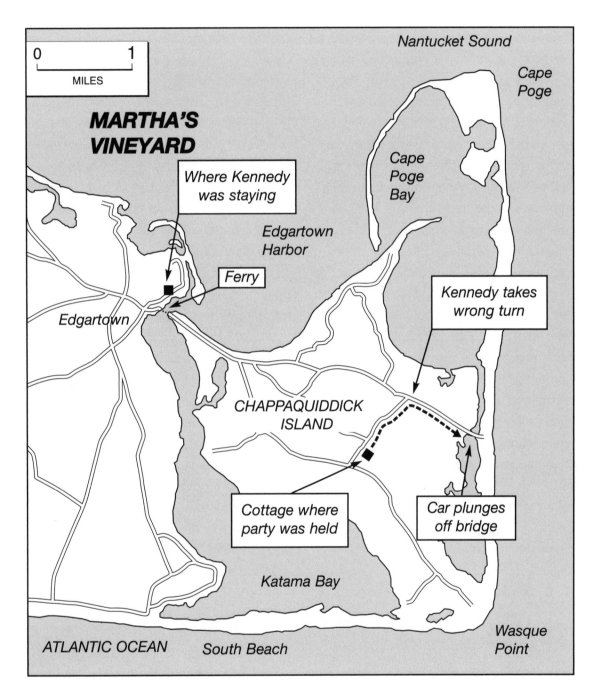

MARTHA'S VINEYARD

Nantucket Sound

Cape Poge

Cape Poge Bay

Where Kennedy was staying

Edgartown Harbor

Ferry

Kennedy takes wrong turn

Edgartown

CHAPPAQUIDDICK ISLAND

Cottage where party was held

Car plunges off bridge

Katama Bay

ATLANTIC OCEAN   South Beach

Wasque Point

appeared to state that the offence should carry a mandatory jail sentence. Throughout the proceedings, Kennedy maintained that he had not been drunk at the time of the accident. By the following day, of course, it was impossible to check whether he was telling the truth or not.

An affair?

Unsurprisingly, many people had a hard time believing Kennedy's version of events and before long evidence began to appear that magnified those doubts. A local Deputy Sheriff, Christopher "Huck" Look, had returned home a little after 12.30 on the night in question and had remembered seeing a car with a man and a woman in it parked close to the point at which the road to the cottage met the main road. Look thought that the occupants might be lost so he got out of his car to offer help. As he approached, the car reversed fast and headed down the road, actually little more than a dirt track, that led to the fateful bridge.

If the car was indeed Kennedy's then the incident casts immediate doubt on the story that he was driving Kopechne to the ferry, because the last boat had left by then. What many suspect is that Kennedy had rather more in mind than a simple lift home for Kopechne and that they were in fact deliberately heading down the dirt road to the nearby beach for a romantic assignation. According to this theory, what then happened was that the appearance of the Sheriff panicked Kennedy, who might well have been intoxicated. This

perhaps caused him to drive too fast down the dirt road so that he ploughed straight off the side of the bridge.

Further doubts have been cast over Kennedy's story that he was too shocked to report the accident. For instance, there were houses near the bridge where he could have asked for help. Instead he made his way to the cottage and called on the assistance of the two men most likely to be discreet, Gargan and Markham. According to Gargan's subsequent testimony, the first thing on Kennedy's mind, even before the fate of Kopechne, was how to cover up his role in the accident. He allegedly told Gargan that they should say that Kopechne herself had been driving the car alone. After Gargan had told him that the plan was potentially disastrous an angered Kennedy then swam off back to his hotel. There he went to bed. He emerged the next day looking fit and well dressed and not at all like a man in shock. It was only when Gargan and Markham came over on the ferry that morning that they persuaded him that he

BELOW: CURIOUS SPECTATORS LOOK ON FROM PIER AT THE CAR DRIVEN BY MASSACHUSETTS SENATOR EDWARD KENNEDY WHICH PLUNGED OFF A BRIDGE ON MARTHA'S VINEYARD ON JULY 19TH.

did indeed have to report the accident.

SUFFOCATED NOT DROWNED

By that time the sunken car had been spotted and diver John Farrar had found the dead body of Kopechne inside. Chillingly, he reported that her posture suggested that she had been caught in an air pocket and had suffocated when the air had run out. She had apparently not drowned. This judgement was allegedly supported by the undertaker who worked on her body, although no autopsy was performed that would have verified the cause of her death. If Farrar was right, however, and Kopechne had been held in an air pocket, it is possible that she may have remained alive for as long as two hours after the crash. In that case it is conceivable that Kennedy's failure to raise the alarm may have brought about her death.

It is harsh, but not unreasonable, to suspect that Kennedy may have valued his career rather more than Kopechne's life. If so, he was only partially successful. The scandal was not enough to force him to resign his Senatorship but it did put paid to his chances of ever becoming president, his greatest ambition.

There are definite elements of conspiracy in the events surrounding the prosecution of the affair. In particular, Kennedy's history of driving offences was mysteriously absent from the records that were given to the court. There are also those who see a larger conspiracy here. These theorists believe that the whole business was a set-up that was designed to discredit Kennedy. According to this theory, the CIA (or perhaps a shadowy organization known as the Power Control Group) had already assassinated John and Robert Kennedy, but realized that it would look too suspicious if they assassinated Edward as well. However, by setting up the Kopechne debacle they might be able to ruin his reputation instead.

The theories get frankly sketchy when a method needs to be found. In essence, they suggest that Kennedy was either drugged at the party or waylaid and knocked out. Then he was taken back to his hotel room unconscious – which explains why he never reported the accident. Meanwhile the CIA drugged or knocked out Kopechne, positioned the car near the bridge, wedged the gas pedal down and launched her to her watery grave. The main problem with this theory is the role of Kennedy himself. On waking up the next morning why wouldn't he have revealed what really happened?

The answer the conspiracy theorists offer is that he was blackmailed, that the CIA threatened to tell his pregnant wife that he was having an affair with Kopechne. This is a pretty thin explanation, however. If Kennedy was so easy to blackmail, there would have been no need to fix up such an elaborate and risky scheme as the one that involved Mary Jo Kopechne. Overall then, it seems likely that the only real conspiracy was the one launched by Kennedy in an attempt to save his career.

THE WACO INCIDENT

Over the past twenty years several events have shaken America and made a significant minority of Americans deeply cynical about the behaviour of their own government. Among the most significant of these is the incident that took place at the Branch Davidian compound near Waco Texas, in early 1993. This culminated in the loss of more than ninety lives as the government appeared to declare war on a tiny religious sect.

The sect in question, the Branch Davidians, were an offshoot of an offshoot of the Seventh Day Adventist Movement. They had been based in a compound called Mount Carmel, outside Waco, Texas since the 1930s. By 1955 the leadership of the group had passed to one Benjamin Roden, who was succeeded in time by his wife Lois. In

1981 a charismatic young man named Vernon Howell joined the group and he soon became a leading light, especially after he began an affair with the much older Lois. A power struggle began between Howell and Lois's son George. George Roden was the initial victor and Howell left the group to start his own splinter group in 1984. Lois died in 1986 and George Roden assumed control for two years until Vernon Howell returned and managed to wrest control back from the increasingly mentally unstable George.

Vernon Howell began to impose his own vision on the sect. He decided that he was a Messiah figure and should be allowed to be polygamous. He was believed to have recruited as many as twelve women as his concubines, some of them the wives of other members and

LEFT: EXPLOSIONS ROCK THE BRANCH DAVIDIAN COMPOUND AT WACO, TEXAS, AS THE FBI AND ATF BEGIN THEIR ASSAULT.

some of them as young as twelve years old. As the Messiah he also exempted himself from the sect's restriction on diet and alcohol. In 1990 he gave himself a new, rather more biblical-sounding, name: David Koresh. His teachings became increasingly apocalyptic with the United States government being denounced continually as Babylonians. The compound was renamed Ranch Apocalypse. The group stockpiled enough food to last for a year as well as large quantities of arms and ammunition. Dealing in guns – legally – also became a significant source of income for the group.

Gradually the activities of the Branch Davidians and their leader started to worry their Texan neighbours. Reports began to appear in the newspapers that Koresh had been accused of abusing children. The Bureau of Alcohol Tobacco and Firearms started taking an interest in their group. When a postman reported a delivery of what appeared to be grenade casings, the investigation intensified and the bureau found evidence of several minor firearms violations.

Rather than simply waiting for Koresh to make one of his regular visits to the city, however, the BATF decided to launch a huge raid on the compound. Scheduled for 28 February 1993 it was meant to be a surprise but news crews had been tipped off and the BATF helicopter flying over the compound shortly beforehand must have warned the residents that something was amiss.

FORCED TO RETREAT

The agents approached the compound that Sunday morning in vehicles disguised as cattle trailers. However, the Branch Davidians were not fooled and the situation very quickly got out of control. As the agents approached the compound, shots rang out. It is still not clear who fired first, with both sides accusing the other, but before long a full-scale gun battle had broken out. By the time the shooting ended four BATF agents and five Branch Davidians were dead and many more were injured.

The BATF had been forced to retreat because they had underestimated the firepower and determination of the sect members. The raid had been an unqualified disaster which had been caught on film for the world to see. Still, the government could not back down now, so a siege began immediately, with the FBI soon taking over the leadership from the BATF. The siege lasted for an amazing fifty-one days. During that time the FBI seemed to employ two distinct tactics. On the one hand, hostage negotiators talked regularly with David Koresh and in the early days of the siege they secured the release of several groups of members, mostly children.

However, although the negotiators were accustomed to hostage situations this one was very different. The remaining people inside the compound did not see themselves as hostages. They were determined to stay with their leader and it became increasingly clear that Koresh was not intending to leave in the near future. At the same time, hostile tactics were also being used. After a while, the electricity was cut off to the compound and later on giant floodlights were trained on the building in order to prevent the occupants from sleeping.

Notoriously, the FBI also played tapes at deafening volume to demoralize the occupants – the sounds on the tapes included Tibetan Buddhist chants, bagpipes, seagulls crying, helicopters, dentists' drills, sirens, dying rabbits, a train and songs by Alice Cooper and Nancy Sinatra. Such tactics had been seen to be useful in the operation against the Panamanian leader General Noriega a couple of years before, but the Branch Davidians seemed to be made of sterner stuff and the FBI started to run out of patience. The operation was enormously expensive and the eyes of the world were upon it. Surely the might of the American government could not be halted by a handful of religious fanatics?

Up in flames

Eventually, Attorney General Janet Reno approved plans for a final assault. This was launched on Monday morning 19 April. The FBI called the compound to warn the occupants that they would be using tear gas. Armed vehicles then approached the compound, punched holes in the walls and sprayed tear gas into the building. Still the Davidians refused to leave. Instead, they started firing at the vehicles. Then the telephone was thrown out, a sign that the talking was over. Later, towards noon, as the FBI pondered its next move, the compound went up in flames. Fires were raging and these were soon punctuated by huge explosions. Finally, nine occupants emerged. One woman came out with her clothing in flames and then tried to go back in, but she was restrained by a BATF agent and taken to safety.

It was too dangerous for firefighters to approach the blaze. Even when it appeared to be in its last stages a soldier was shot at when he approached the building. Eventually, however, the compound was razed to the ground and the FBI was able to inspect the damage. They found eighty dead bodies amongst the rubble of which twenty-three were children (fourteen of whom were fathered by Koresh). The body of Koresh himself was identified by his dental records. He had been shot in the head.

This was an operation that had gone about as wrong as it possibly could. The FBI tried to stress that the Branch Davidians had set the fires themselves and so had committed mass suicide, but it was inevitable that the conspiracy theorists would soon get to work.

Deliberate murder?

Essentially the conspiracy theorists were all saying the same thing, that the FBI had deliberately murdered the Branch

Davidians. Evidence for this, however, was at first slight but the dogged investigations of a right-wing maverick named Michael McNulty started to raise embarrassing questions. He would air his findings in two successful films about the affair – the Academy Award nominated *Waco: The Rules Of Engagement* and *Waco: A New Revelation*.

Two key allegations are made by McNulty. The first is that the FBI caused the fires. After the event, the FBI had always maintained that it had not used any flammable substance or weapon in its assault on the compound. McNulty discovered, however, that flammable tear gas canisters had been used in the attack. The FBI finally reversed its earlier statements and admitted this in 1999. Secondly, McNulty examined heat-sensitive film of the operation and noticed flashes coming from behind the building. These, he claimed, were muzzle flashes – proof that the FBI had been firing on anyone trying to escape the fire.

Some of McNulty's other charges were supported by rather less documentary evidence. They included the suggestion that soldiers from the Army's super-secret Delta Force participated in the attack; that hand-held grenade launchers were fired at the kitchen and could have ignited the fire; and that a demolition charge was placed on the roof of the bunker which was detonated by remote control.

So how has the FBI responded to these charges? The explosion in the bunker has been blamed on the quantity of arms possessed by the occupants. The use of grenade launchers and the active involvement of Delta Force soldiers (though they were acknowledged to have been present) were both flatly denied. The flashes on the heat- resistant film were written off as reflected sunlight, with experts pointing out that a muzzle would have to be attached to a human being who would also show up on heat-resistant

film. As for the flammable CS gas canisters, the FBI says that they were launched four hours prior to the fire breaking out but, in any case, they had failed to reach their target. This was backed up by a civil jury, Congress, the Court and the Special Counsel who, in the year 2000, all concluded that the FBI had not caused the fire. The FBI also point out they had introduced bugging devices into the compound which clearly recorded cult members spreading fuel about and preparing to light it.

TRAGIC CONSEQUENCES

All this, of course, has cut little ice with conspiracy theorists. What they and many other Americans point out was that here was a religious group surrounded by government forces but still going up in flames. The Waco incident made for potent TV images and proved a powerful recruiting aid for the far-right militias. This incident would bear terrible fruit two years later when, on the anniversary of the Waco deaths, a young man named Timothy McVeigh decided to take vengeance on the government by perpetrating the Oklahoma City bombing.

So, do the conspiracists have a point? Could Waco have been a massive plot by the government against its own people? It seems unlikely, because in the final analysis there is no reason why the government would have actively wanted to bring about the annihilation of this obscure religious cult. What seems far more likely is that this was simply a disastrously badly handled affair. It was less a conspiracy than a shambles. Unfortunately, however, the consequences of the government's actions were tragic, both in the short and the long term.

Mind Control: MKULTRA

One of the most bizarre and disturbing conspiracies of all time was Project MKULTRA. This was the secret name for a series of CIA experiments that took place from the 1950s to the 1970s, which were designed to explore the possibilities of mind control through the use of drugs such as LSD and mescaline. In these experiments, subjects were given mind-altering drugs, often without their prior knowledge, and their subsequent behaviour was then studied.

In several cases the experiments resulted in the death of one or another of the participants and there were many instances of severe, permanently damaging mental illness. However, the CIA continued to conduct the trials until the project was finally exposed. Ultimately, very little useful information about mind control resulted from MKULTRA and it seems that sadism, rather than serious scientific enquiry, was the driving force behind some of the experiments.

Truth drugs

MKULTRA was set up by Allen Dulles, head of the CIA, in 1953, in order to look into the use of mind control techniques. The project was led by Dr Sidney Gottleib, and early research was directed towards trying to find a "truth drug" for use in the interrogation of Russian spies. The project was wide reaching, with over a hundred research programmes, many of which were secret, and experiments were conducted on army and other personnel without their knowledge.

In the initial phase of the project, the effect of radiation on the human mind was the main focus of research but, as time went on, interest began to centre on the effect of psychotropic drugs, particularly LSD. As the programmes proliferated, subjects began to be recruited from outside the army and the CIA. Patients

DOCTOR TIMOTHY LEARY, ACID GURU AND MAIN ADVOCATE OF THE USE OF LSD TO GAIN INSIGHT INTO THE WORLD BEYOND THE SENSES.

ABOVE: MICHAEL CAINE STARS IN *THE IPCRESS FILE*, A SPY THRILLER IN WHICH MIND CONTROL THROUGH THE USE OF DRUGS FEATURES HEAVILY.

with mental illnesses (many of them with minor disorders such as mild depression and anxiety), prostitutes and other types of individual were often used as guinea pigs. An undeniable element of torture crept into the experiments, as Gottleib began to tie his victims up in straitjackets after administering the drugs. They were often locked them in rooms where they could see or hear nothing or tape loops were played to them in an attempt to drive them mad. Gottleib also ordered his subjects to be given enormous amounts of LSD – in one experiment, volunteers were given the drug for a period of over two months, causing many of them to suffer permanent mental damage.

OPERATION MIDNIGHT CLIMAX

As time went on, the MKULTRA research programmes became ever more bizarre and unpleasant, but they yielded very little in the way of scientific results. One of the most infamous of the experiments was Operation Midnight Climax, in which Dr

George Hunter White recruited prostitutes from San Francisco. The prostitutes were asked to administer LSD to their clients without the clients' knowledge. The LSD was put into the victims' drinks and CIA operatives monitored their behaviour through two-way mirrors. No scientific benefits at all accrued from this experiment – the operatives were not trained scientists – and one can only assume that it was set up as a means of satisfying the prurient interests of those who devised it. However, it took more than a decade for this programme to end.

It was later revealed that Dr Gottleib's behaviour as head of MKULTRA was also questionable. He was known to take large amounts of LSD himself and he seemed obsessed with the drug, even though it began to emerge that it was of very little use as a mind control device. Subjects under the influence of the drug behaved erratically and, if anything, became less susceptible to interrogation than they had been without the drug.

DANGEROUS TREATMENTS

Undeterred by the fact that LSD seemed

to be useless as a mind-controlling substance, the MKULTRA team went on to perform more and more dangerous experiments on their hapless victims. In some cases, they simultaneously drip-fed a mixture of amphetamines and barbiturates into their subjects, which resulted in extreme mental confusion and sometimes even death. In addition to the use of LSD, amphetamines, and barbiturates the MKULTRA team experimented with other drugs such as heroin, mescaline, marijuana and alcohol.

Perhaps the worst abuses of all took place in Canada, under the aegis of Dr Ewan Cameron. Dr Cameron had put forward a theory of "psychic driving" in which he claimed that the mind could be erased and then corrected through drugs and other therapies. He conducted experiments in Montreal over a period of almost a decade, using a combination of electroconvulsive therapy and drugs, both administered at well above the normal levels. He regularly induced comas in his subjects, sometimes for months on end, while playing them tape loops, supposedly to correct their thinking. Not surprisingly, by the end of his treatment, many of his patients were mentally scarred for life.

BLOWING THE WHISTLE

It was not until 1974 that the project came under press scrutiny, when an article in The New York Times reported on the CIA's history of experimentation on human beings for the purposes of "mind control" research. Several committees were set up to look into what had happened, but they found that much of the evidence had gone missing. Many of MKULTRA's records had been destroyed in order to prevent the truth from ever coming out. Even so, there was enough information to show that the MKULTRA project had been very extensive. Over thirty universities and other institutions had been involved and many of the subjects had been completely unaware that they were being given drugs. Not only this, but the experiments were mostly completely pointless from a scientific point of view.

It was also revealed that an army scientist, Frank Olsen, had been given LSD without his knowledge as part of an experiment and had later thrown himself out of a window and died. His family later alleged that he was murdered because he knew too much about the CIA's nefarious activities. There were also reports that a professional tennis player, Harold Blauer, had died as a result of being given high doses of mescaline without his consent.

Following these revelations, the United States army was also investigated and a number of shocking cases came to light in which subjects had been given drugs without their consent or knowledge, as a part of so-called experiments. Legislation was enacted to prevent such abuses occurring again and compensation was paid to some of the victims. Nevertheless, the MKULTRA project remains one of the most sinister, and bizarre, state conspiracies ever to have taken place in America, or perhaps anywhere else.

CHAPTER SIX:

FROM AGATHA CHRISTIE'S GENTEEL CRIMINALS, TO THE MORE GRAPHIC DETECTIVE NOVELS OF THE TWENTY-FIRST CENTURY, A GOOD MURDER MYSTERY IS THE BOOK OF CHOICE WITH WHICH TO CURL UP IN AN ARMCHAIR.

MURDER MYSTERIES

FOR MILLIONS OF PEOPLE THE WORLD OVER. AND IF
THAT MURDER MYSTERY INVOLVES CELEBRITIES, SEX,
POLITICIANS, AND MAY IN FACT BE TRUE, THAT ONLY
SERVES TO MAKE IT ALL THE MORE ENJOYABLE!

WHO SHOT JFK?

The assassination of John F. Kennedy on 22 November 1963 has generated more conspiracy theories than almost any other crime in history. This is partly because the crime was such a shocking, dramatic event. As we all know, the President was fatally shot in full view of the public while riding along in an open-topped motorcade, with his wife beside him. But it is also because the hastily assembled Warren Commission, set up just one week after the assassination for the purpose of enquiring into what happened, failed to account for the many perplexing aspects

of the crime. The Commission found that a lone gunman, Lee Harvey Oswald, had fired three shots at the President. The first of these missed the motorcade; the second wounded both Kennedy and the Governor of Texas, John B. Connally, who was also riding in the limousine; and the third and final shot hit Kennedy in the head, killing him.

The related conspiracy theories became known as "The Lone Gunman Theory" and "The Single Bullet Theory" (often jokingly referred to as the "Magic Bullet Theory" because it seemed so

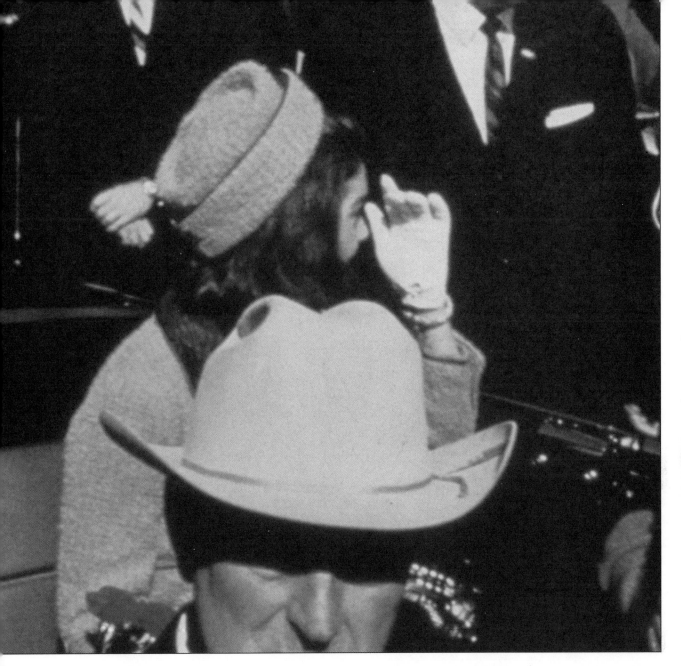

ABOVE: THE MOST FAMOUS CONSPIRACY OF ALL: PRESIDENT JOHN F. KENNEDY AND WIFE JACKIE IN THE LIMOUSINE THAT WOULD TAKE KENNEDY TO HIS DEATH ON DEALEY PLAZA, DALLAS.

unlikely that one bullet could penetrate two people). In time, both theories came to be regarded as highly implausible – not only by the experts but by the majority of the American public, who were polled on numerous occasions in order to obtain their opinions on the matter.

To compound the confusions, on 24 November 1963 Jack Ruby, a Dallas nightclub owner , shot Oswald dead while he was in police captivity. Once again, the killing took place in full view of the public. The event prompted a new wave of speculation. How was it that Ruby had

found it so easy to flout the tight security surrounding Oswald? Had Oswald been swiftly executed in order to prevent incriminating evidence being brought against establishment figures at the trial? And what about Ruby's links to the world of organized crime? Was the Mafia involved in some way with Kennedy's death? Ruby swore that he had been acting on his own, in revenge for the killing, but many disbelieved him. By the time he died of a stroke on 3 January 1967, his motives were still thought by some to be questionable.

THE GRASSY KNOLL

Rumours about the Kennedy assassination persisted throughout the years that followed until, in 1976, the evidence was re-examined by a House Select Committee that was convened for that purpose. This time, the committee found that there were probably two gunmen, not one, and that four bullets were fired: three by Oswald, and one from an unknown gunman hiding in a nearby area that was known as the Grassy Knoll. Many witness reports were collected, some of them conflicting, and evidence

ABOVE: FIRST LADY JACQUELINE KENNEDY LEANS OVER TO ASSIST HER HUSBAND JUST AFTER HE IS SHOT AS THE PRESIDENTIAL MOTORCADE PASSES THROUGH DEALEY PLAZA, DALLAS, 22 NOVEMBER, 1963.

was also acquired from people who had photographed, filmed, or recorded the event. However, the report was not conclusive. It merely suggested that a conspiracy of some kind seemed likely, given the probability that two gunmen were responsible (a theory based on acoustic recordings of the gunshots fired).

A case of foul play?

After the assassination, many troubling facts surrounding the event came to light. For example, the limousine that the President had been travelling in was taken away and cleaned up directly after the shooting, rather than being preserved so that forensic examinations could take place. Also, Kennedy's body should have been inspected by the local coroner according to Texan law, but it was immediately taken to Washington instead. Moreover, the area in which the assassination had taken place, The Dealey Plaza, should have been sealed off by police. The place where Oswald worked, the Texas School Book Depository, should have been closed off also. However, in the event neither place was secured, so vital clues to what really happened might well have been lost. And later, important pieces of evidence were found to be missing, such as the hat that Governor Connally was holding in his hand when he was shot, and the cufflink from his shirt. More shockingly, photographs of Kennedy's autopsy also disappeared.

Much of this, of course, could be put down to official incompetence but, after the assassination, there were so many anomalies surrounding the event that a host of conspiracy theories arose to explain what had actually happened. Some of these – like the idea that Kennedy masterminded his own suicide – are difficult to credit. Others, however, such as the theory that right-wing elements of the American establishment wanted Kennedy out of the way, and therefore arranged the shooting, do not seem altogether implausible.

The rival strikes

One of the most compelling theories regarding the assassination of Kennedy concerns his political role. At the time, the Cold War had preserved an uneasy truce between the two superpowers, the USA and the USSR, and many thought that it played an essential part in preserving the status quo and preventing nuclear war. In some quarters, Kennedy was seen as a loose cannon, a young idealistic president who could not be relied upon to maintain a strong stance in the face of Soviet aggression. The Cuban Missile Crisis, in which the USSR and the USA had come close to an all-out nuclear conflict, had shown how important it was to maintain a balance between the two sides and what the consequences of any change in the status quo might be.

American foreign policy at the time – which later turned out to be disastrous – was to escalate America's "anti-communist" involvement in Vietnam. Kennedy had shown signs of pulling back

ABOVE: LEE HARVEY OSWALD IS ASSASSINATED BY NIGHTCLUB OWNER JACK RUBY AT DALLAS POLICE STATION, 24 NOVEMBER, 1963

from the conflict by recalling United States forces and questioning the scale of human losses that would inevitably ensue. Thus, Kennedy was beginning to be seen as a liability within the political establishment. Conversely, his Vice President, Lydon B. Johnson, appeared to offer a safe pair of hands. He was older, more pragmatic and apparently impervious to the liberal currents running through America during the 1960s.

When Johnson took over, he immediately sent troops back to Vietnam and stepped up anti-communist political propaganda in the United States. The speedy change in foreign and domestic policy confirmed to some observers that the political establishment were behind Kennedy's killing. Oswald was thought to be a decoy figure, a pro-communist who

had been hired to shoot the President so that Johnson could take over. The extent of Johnson's personal involvement in the plot remained unclear, but some believed that he had arranged the shooting himself. It also transpired that shortly before he died Kennedy had been thinking of removing Johnson from office, mainly because the Vice President was the subject of four criminal investigations (all of which were dropped after he became the new President). Johnson had more than enough motive to arrange the assassination, it seemed.

MAFIA MADNESS

Another theory was that President Kennedy was killed by the Mafia. The Kennedy regime had made it a priority to crack down on organized crime and high-level Mafia leaders were being prosecuted for illegal activities such as gambling, drug running, racketeering and pimping. There was particular resentment among some Mafia bosses, as they had directed Mafia-

DURING THE VIETNAM WAR, KENNEDY BEGAN TO BE SEEN BY SOME AS A POLITICAL LIABILITY

linked organizations, such as workers' unions, to run campaigns supporting Kennedy's election. Because they expected to be protected from prosecution once he was in power, so the theory goes, Kennedy's war on organized crime was seen as a betrayal and so he was gunned down in revenge.

It was significant that Jack Ruby, who shot Oswald, had worked for Al Capone as a young man and had continued to be part of the world of organized crime.

According to this theory, Oswald was hired to shoot the President so that it would seem that a communist had done the deed. Oswald was then shot by Ruby, who was posing as a loyal citizen. In this way, Oswald's testimony would not be heard and it would not emerge that it was the Mafia, and not the communists, who had shot one of America's most popular presidents.

Finally, commentators noted that prosecutions of Mafia organizations returned to their normal level after the assassination of Kennedy.

A CIA PLOT?
Not only the Mafia but the CIA had strong reasons to get Kennedy out of the way. Once in office, Kennedy infuriated the agency by refusing to back the Bay of Pigs invasion in Cuba, which was part of a plot to overthrow the Communist leader Fidel Castro. Kennedy sacked the Director of the CIA, Alan Dulles, and there were constant run-ins between the President and the agency, especially after the failed invasion of Cuba.

The CIA worked closely with the Mafia, and both organizations saw it as mutually beneficial to oust Castro from Cuba. The CIA's motive was to rid the United States of their closest communist neighbour and the Mafia's motive was to win back control of the organized crime business in Cuba, which they had lost when Castro took control. Several top Mafia men, aided by the CIA, plotted to assassinate Castro. Thus, Kennedy's perceived reluctance to support their anti-Cuban stance was a constant source of irritation to the CIA and the Mafia.

THE FBI BOSS
The head of the FBI, J. Edgar Hoover, was also suspected of plotting Kennedy's assassination. There was a good deal of mutual animosity between Hoover and the Kennedy clan. Hoover and Johnson, on the other hand, were the best of friends. Hoover was coming up to retirement age and he knew that Kennedy would let him go whereas Johnson, by contrast, would keep him in. Commentators noted that after Johnson became president, he did indeed retain Hoover's services as head of the FBI – "for life".

THE OTHER CONTENDERS
There are many other theories regarding the culprits in the Kennedy assassination: some of them simple, others labyrinthine. First, there are the "economic issue" conspiracy theories. For example, some think that the oil barons wanted the

President dead because he had changed the tax laws regarding oil, which would lose them enormous profits. Others suppose that officials of the US central bank, the Federal Reserve, were worried by the President's plans to stop the counterfeiting of money by backing the currency with precious metals.

Then there are the "political issue" hypotheses. Castro was behind the assassination, it has been said, as a response to the constant attempts by

FOR MANY, KENNEDY'S DEATH WAS A PERSONAL TRAGEDY

United States agents to murder him. Another theory is that followers of the South Vietnam President, Ngo Dinh Diem, ordered the assassination in revenge for his death after the United States plotted a coup against him. Others say that Kennedy was a puppet of the Soviet Union, which then turned against him.

The following theories are more implausible, in the eyes of most people. The first one states that Kennedy was killed in order to avenge the honour of Jacqueline Kennedy, to whom he had been unfaithful on many occasions. Another suggests that Aristotle Onassis ordered Kennedy's murder, along with his friends in the secret Illuminati cabal. Finally, some people imagine that Kennedy did not die at all, but that the whole event was somehow stage-managed to look as though he did. To support this theory, an exchange of bodies would need to have taken place at the autopsy.

Whatever the truth of the matter, some people consider that the Warren Commission's initial findings were questionable and that there were strong pressures to rid the country of a president that threatened to shake up the status quo, both within the government and outside it. Perhaps President Kennedy acted through inexperience and recklessness, as some critics believed, or maybe he had made a serious moral commitment to rid the US of the atmosphere of distrust and fear that had built up as a result of the Cold War, both in terms of domestic and of foreign policy.

For many, Kennedy's death was seen as a tragedy. Whatever his personal failings, he stood as a symbol of hope for a better, more peaceable world, not only for America but for many other countries too. On the day he was killed there were hundreds of troops flying back from Vietnam on his express orders. Had he gone on to withdraw entirely from Vietnam, the Vietnamese and the American public might have been spared one of the most appalling wars in recent history. No wonder, then, that so many intelligent, committed political analysts refuse to let the matter drop and continue to ask to this day: who shot JFK?

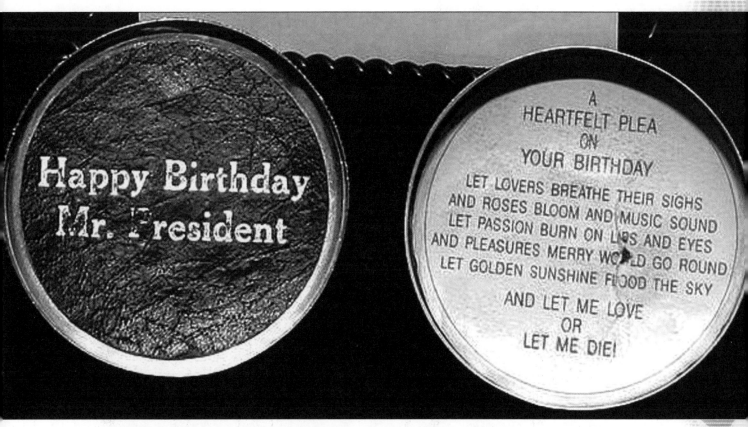

MARILYN MONROE: SUICIDE OR MURDER?

At first sight it seemed simple enough. A famous movie actress, whose career was on the skids, took an overdose and died. She had enjoyed a famously turbulent love life and she had a history of suicide attempts. A sad but familiar end to a celebrity's life. That's what the coroner's verdict would ultimately conclude.

An open and shut case? Not really. From the very start there were worrying circumstances. When Monroe's body was found, where was the glass of water she would surely have needed if she had swallowed an overdose of sleeping

tablets? And why did her body look as if it had been neatly arranged – quite unlike the usual posture of overdose victims? Why the delay in calling the police and the ambulance? Could it have been to do with the phone calls she made and received on the last evening of her life, including one to the actor and Kennedy intimate Peter Lawford? And was it true that Robert Kennedy, younger brother of President Jack Kennedy, had been seen driving his

ABOVE: ROLEX WATCH GIVEN TO JOHN F. KENNEDY BY MARILYN MONROE, INSCRIBED WITH THE 'HEARTFELT PLEA': 'LET ME LOVE OR LET ME DIE!'

ABOVE: DURING A PARTY AT THE HOME OF MOVIE EXECUTIVE ARTHUR KRIM, MARILYN MONROE STANDS BETWEEN ROBERT KENNEDY (LEFT) AND JOHN F. KENNEDY.

car away from her house that night?

MONROE'S LOVE AFFAIRS

Rumours about what had been going on in Monroe's life before she died abounded, and it was only a matter of time before several competing conspiracy theories began to surface. Most of them centred on her involvement with the President. According to these accounts, Monroe had been having an affair with John F. Kennedy and had threatened to go public on the subject, which would have destroyed Kennedy's political career. Clearly, in those circumstances, the President would have had every reason to have her silenced.

No one suggested that J.F. Kennedy had actually killed Marilyn Monroe with his own hands, so the next step was to determine the identity of the killer. Some named the President's brother, Robert Kennedy. Various witnesses claimed to have seen him visit Monroe during the course of the fatal evening. Could he have gone to plead his brother's case and then – when she refused to stay silent – did he resort to killing her?

Another theory also claims that Robert Kennedy murdered Monroe but that he did not commit the act on his brother's behalf but his own, because he too was having an affair with Monroe. This theory suffers from a lack of evidence and some argue that, even if the two had been lovers, there would have been less for Robert to lose if Marilyn had decided to go public and reveal the liaison.

Mafia men

It was then suggested that the murderer was a hireling of gangster Sam Giancana. According to this theory, Kennedy had turned to his Mafia boss friend for help in the delicate situation he found himself in. Giancana then gladly agreed to send his henchmen in to deal with Monroe. In return, Kennedy was to assist Giancana with projects that were dear to the Mafia's heart, such as the overthrow of Fidel Castro.

As with Robert Kennedy, there were those who suspected that Giancana could have carried out the murder on his own behalf, in a bid to silence Monroe because they had been having an affair. However, as many have pointed out, if it had been revealed that a mobster had been having an affair with Marilyn Monroe it could only have enhanced his reputation!

Since Monroe's death, the many conspiracy theories that have been advanced have mostly been met with scepticism. Most people are reluctant to believe that the President of the United States, or his brother, could have murdered a legendary movie star in order to protect their reputations. However, it does seem that in the case of Monroe's death – as in the case of the assassination of Kennedy himself – there are plenty of disturbing facts and questions that still

need to be answered. Reputable Monroe biographers such as Anthony Summers and Donald Spoto have tended to steer a middle course, suggesting that her death was neither a deliberate murder nor an innocent suicide, but something rather more complex than that.

An accidental overdose?

It is possible that Monroe's death was the result of an accidental overdose. She had been taking a great many prescription drugs at the time. Her preferred drug administration method was by enema. So it is possible that she received the fatal overdose in this form, perhaps administered by her housekeeper, Eunice Murray. This would explain the fact that there were few drugs in her bloodstream after her death. However, it seems unlikely that anyone would choose to murder her in this way.

The most plausible scenario seems to be that Monroe was indeed having an affair with the President, but was devastated when he broke the affair off and committed suicide as a reaction. Then, whoever discovered her dead body – whether it was her housekeeper or Robert Kennedy – panicked, moved things around in the room and delayed calling the authorities. Not a murder, then, but a scandal and a cover-up.

Finally, though, this is one of those cases where it seems unlikely that things will ever be conclusively proven either way. Suicide or murder? The choice is yours – and there are plenty of accounts

THE ASSASSINATION OF MALCOLM X

At the time of his assassination on 21 February 1965, Malcolm X was one of the two leading black political figures in America. The other was Martin Luther King, who was himself assassinated just a couple of years later. However, where Martin Luther King was a broadly popular figure, a man of the church with a commitment to non-violent change, Malcolm was seen as a much more threatening figure. White liberals hailed Martin Luther King as the leader of the civil rights movement. On the other hand, Malcolm X was treated with suspicion because he was the main spokesman for a group called the Nation of Islam – commonly known as the Black Muslims – who were overtly anti-white and rather less inclined to turn the other cheek.

During the early sixties, Malcolm, a former petty criminal who had discovered the Nation Of Islam while in prison, became a hate figure in the mainstream American media and was routinely vilified for his anti-white statements. During the last year of his life, however, he began to travel more, especially to Africa, and after meeting anti-apartheid activists in South Africa he became convinced that black and white people could work together to achieve political change. This realization caused him to split with the Nation Of Islam and during the summer of 1964 he formed his own group, the Organization of Afro-American Unity.

Shortly after forming this organization Malcolm X returned to Africa for a period of several months, finally returning to the United States in November 1964. While he was in Africa he continually complained that he was being followed by CIA agents. In Cairo he was seriously ill, perhaps as the result of having his food poisoned. Things were no better when he returned to the United States. Over the next few months a feud developed between Malcolm and the Nation Of Islam, the group he had resigned from. Death threats were issued against him.

HOUSE FIREBOMBED

A week before his eventual assassination Malcolm's house in Queens, New York was firebombed. At the time Malcolm assumed that the Nation Of Islam was behind the attack. The following day, 15 February, Malcolm made a speech at the Audubon Ballroom in Harlem. As he spoke a scuffle broke out in the audience. Six days later Malcolm returned to the Audubon. Mysteriously, all the other speakers that were scheduled to appear cancelled their engagements. While Malcolm was waiting to speak he allegedly confided to friends in the backstage area

RIGHT: MALCOLM X RECOGNIZED THE IMMENSE POWER OF THE PRESS AND USED IT ASSIDUOUSLY IN PROMOTING HIMSELF AND HIS ORGANIZATION THE NATION OF ISLAM.

Faubus Deplores Deaths of Boys
ARKANSAS BURIES HER 21 VICTIMS OF FLAMES
Courier
NEW YORK
Amsterdam New
Jury Deadlocks, Mistrial Called
Moslems Go Fre
Louis Remarries
Trial For Couple
NAACP Member Ca
'Credit' In Teacher T
31st
New Jersey
Herald News
N. Y. Moslems Pack Courtroom
In "Invasion Of Privacy" Tes
The Political Pot
For Hawaiian Islands Blow To The South
NEW YORK AGE
Protest 'Police Brutality'
ACCUSED BY MOSLEMS
Moslem Followers Mass At Courthouse
BROOKLYN
Amsterdam News
Moslems' Ten
Moslems

ABOVE: MALCOLM X RETURNING HOME ON THE 14 FEBRUARY 1965 AFTER HIS HOUSE WAS FIRE-BOMBED. THERE WERE MANY SUSPECTS FOR THE CRIME, BUT NOTHING WAS EVER PROVEN IN COURT.

During the chaos, a black man came towards the stage and shot Malcolm in the chest at point-blank range.

that he was not sure that it had been the Nation Of Islam after all that had been behind the firebombing. Then he went onstage and began to give his speech.

At around 3.05 p.m. Eastern Standard Time a disturbance broke out in the crowd of 400. A man yelled, "Get your hand outta my pocket! Don't be messin' with my pockets!" Then a smoke bomb went off at the back of the auditorium causing confusion. Malcolm's bodyguards moved forward to calm the crowd but meanwhile, taking advantage of the chaos, a black man came towards the stage and shot Malcolm in the chest at point-blank range with a sawn-off shotgun. Two other men quickly charged towards the stage and fired handguns at Malcolm. The three assassins attempted to escape, but the angry crowd managed to capture one of the two men with handguns, one Talmadge Hayer.

Malcolm's bodyguard Gene Roberts, actually an undercover cop, attempted to resuscitate Malcolm but to no avail. Malcolm was dead. The autopsy was performed by New York City's Chief Medical Examiner, Dr. Milton Helpern, and it was discovered that "the cause of death was multiple shotgun pellet and bullet

wounds in the chest, heart and aorta". Malcolm had been hit by eight shotgun slugs and nine bullets.

Malcolm's funeral was held in Harlem on 27 February 1965 at the Faith Temple Church of God in Christ (now Child's Memorial Temple Church of God in Christ). The ceremony was attended by 1,500 people. Malcolm X was buried at the Ferncliff Cemetery in Hartsdale, New York, where his friends took the shovels away from the waiting gravediggers and buried him themselves. Soon, three people were arrested for his murder. They were Nation of Islam members Talmadge Hayer, Norman 3X Butler, and Thomas 15X Johnson. All three were convicted of first-degree murder in March 1966.

On the face of it, this was an open and shut case, the result of infighting between black radicals. The Nation Of Islam had murdered their greatest ex-member. The mainstream media either said good riddance or shed crocodile tears. And moved on. Gradually, though, suspicions began to circulate that all may not have been as it seemed.

A cover-up?
Suspicion centred around the notion that

Malcolm might have been murdered by his fellow black men who had been manipulated: they could have believed that they were carrying out the wishes of the Nation of Islam.

It was not hard to find fuel for those suspicions. Even in the immediate aftermath of the murder a police source had told the *Herald Tribune* that "several" members of the highly secretive Bureau of Special Services (BOSS) were present in the audience at the time of the killing. One suggest that his co-defendants were not even at the Audubon Ballroom at the time, and that the two other killers have never been brought to justice. As for Talmadge Hayer, he has stated that he was not a member of the Nation of Islam and "that the man who hired him was not a Muslim" either, according to a 1971 book, *The Assassination of Malcolm X.*

So was it the government or the Nation Of Islam that was really behind the murder. There is a suspicion of government

WHETHER OR NOT THE STATE WAS INVOLVED, IT IS PROBABLY TRUE TO SAY THAT FEW AT THE FBI SHED MANY TEARS FOR MALCOLM X.

of those undercover cops, Gene Roberts, was one of Malcolm X's bodyguards at the time he was killed.

On 25 February 1965, four days after the assassination of Malcolm X, one of his senior lieutenants at the OAAU, Leon 4X Ameer, announced that he was convinced that his life was in danger. Less than three weeks later, he died of an apparent overdose of sleeping pills. It is alleged that he had been on the point of revealing evidence of government involvement in Malcolm's murder.

Further speculation surrounds the question of who really carried out the killing. Talmadge Hayer was certainly guilty, but there is plenty of evidence to involvement here, and it is probably true to say that few people at the FBI shed many tears for Malcolm X. On the other hand, the Nation of Islam was locked in a struggle with Malcolm and its leading lights like Elijah Muhammad, and his eventual successor Louis Farrakhan did publicly call for Malcolm's elimination. It might well be that both parties are implicated. Perhaps the killers were Black Muslims and they were egged on by agents provocateurs. Whatever the truth behind the killing, the inescapable fact is that another great sixties leader was cut down in his prime, like John F. Kennedy before him and Martin Luther King not long afterwards.

THE DEATH OF PRINCESS DIANA

In the early hours of Sunday, 31 August 1997, news of the death of Princess Diana shocked the world. She and her lover Dodi Al-Fayed had been killed in a car crash as they sped through a Paris tunnel during the night. The driver of the car, Henri Paul, was also killed and Diana's bodyguard, Trevor Rees Jones, was seriously injured.

At first, the cause of the accident seemed straightforward enough. In an attempt to shake off the paparazzi who were pursuing the couple on motorcycles, the driver had taken the car down into the tunnel just a little too fast and had ended up smacking into one of the pillars inside it. But then, questions began to be asked. Why was the car travelling so fast? Had Henri Paul been drinking? If so, why had he been allowed to drive the car of Britain's number one celebrity, Princess Diana, whose doomed marriage to the heir to the throne, Prince Charles, had generated pages of speculation and scandal in the worldwide press for over a

BELOW: THE PLAN TO KILL DIANA? BRITISH NEWSPAPERS REPORTING THE STORY THAT DIANA BELIEVED THE ROYAL FAMILY WANTED HER OUT OF THE WAY SO THAT PRINCE CHARLES COULD MARRY AGAIN.

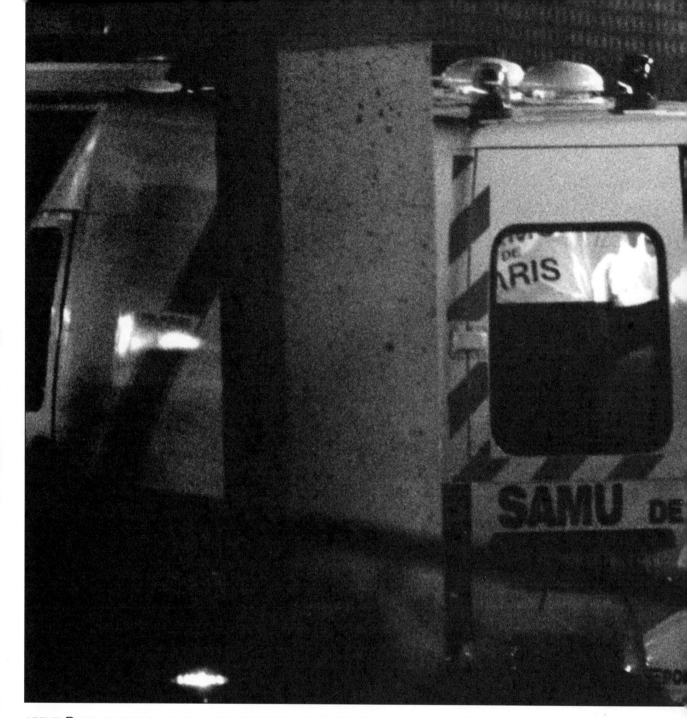

ABOVE: DIANA IS LOADED – ALIVE – INTO AN AMBULANCE IN THE PARIS UNDERPASS. QUESTIONS ARE ASKED ABOUT THE LENGTH OF TIME THE AMBULANCE TOOK TO MAKE THE JOURNEY TO THE HOSPITAL.

decade. Why had the lights in the tunnel, and the security cameras, apparently failed just before the crash? Why had it taken so long for Princess Diana, who was still alive after the crash, to be taken to hospital by ambulance?

And, after her death from cardiac arrest in the hospital, why was her body immediately embalmed, before a post-mortem could be undertaken? Had she been pregnant? Was it possible that MI6 and the British royal family wanted her –

and her lover, son of one of Britain's richest businessmen, Mohammed Al-Fayed – out of the way? Had the Princess's indiscretions – her affairs, her criticism of the royal family, her increasingly eccentric behaviour – earned her enemies in high places? Al-Fayed senior claimed that the couple had been murdered, that they had been planning to marry and that the British establishment had decided that it was time to get them out of the way.

At first, Al-Fayed's claim was seen as paranoid but as time went on and more anomalies in the case surfaced, the theory began to seem less outlandish. Soon, others began to be convinced that this was no ordinary accident but a case of foul play.

Did MI6 kill Diana?

Initially, the press reported the tragic event as a car crash caused by the fact that Henri Paul, the driver, had simply made a mistake. But it then began to emerge that Paul, a security officer at the Ritz hotel,

was an experienced and careful driver who had taken driving courses in the past. Not only this, but the car was only travelling at about sixty or seventy miles per hour, not at a hundred and twenty as had at first been reported. Next, there were allegations that Paul had been drunk at the wheel, but security cameras at the hotel showed that he was acting in a perfectly normal way minutes before taking the wheel. Moreover, he was unlikely to have been drinking when on call to such important hotel guests as Princess Diana and Dodi Al-Fayed. Later, it was found that even before they took samples of his blood the police had in fact announced that Paul was drunk.

So, if the car was not going too fast and Paul was not drunk, why had the accident happened? Conflicting reports by some witnesses told of a car blocking the way so that Paul had to turn off his normal route into the tunnel and of cycles ramming the car as it travelled along, causing it to swerve. Some suggested that Paul had been in the pay of MI6, that he had been hired to kill Princess Diana and Dodi and that something had gone wrong at the last minute so that he ended up killing himself as well. What was odd, and is still unexplained, is why Dodi asked Paul to drive the couple home instead of using his usual driver, Philippe Junot.

The fatal moment

According to some reports, all the lights in the tunnel went out shortly before the car approached, and the security cameras in the tunnel also failed. On this evidence, a theory has been constructed that Paul was used as a dupe, and that the French authorities deliberately arranged for the car to crash, thus killing the inmates. It has even been suggested that Rees Jones was somehow in on the plot because he survived, protected by his safety belt when Princess Diana and Dodi were not wearing theirs. However, his involvement is somewhat implausible. Deliberately travelling in a car that is destined to have a fatal accident seems a little too risky a strategy – even for a man trained by the Parachute Regiment, one of the toughest regiments in the British army.

What does emerge as odd, however, is how the French authorities responded at the scene of the accident. In the immediate minutes after the crash, Diana appeared not to be seriously harmed. It later emerged that she was suffering from internal bleeding, but to the off-duty doctor who arrived first on the scene, Frederick Mailliez, she did not appear to be in a fatal condition. As she clearly needed medical attention, an ambulance was called but, strangely, it took it over an hour to get to the hospital. It even stopped on the way for ten minutes! Afterwards, it was explained that the ambulance had stopped in order to administer a shot of adrenalin to the princess and that it had travelled slowly to avoid jolting her.

However, many remain unconvinced by this and they still cannot understand why Princess Diana was taken to a hospital some distance away, when there were

several nearby that could have attended to her. After all, this was no ordinary car crash victim. This was Diana, the Princess of Wales, one of the most famous and recognizable women on the planet.

Not only that, but important evidence was also cleared away from the scene of the accident immediately after the victims had been taken to hospital. Within just a few hours, the tunnel had been cleaned and disinfected and it was soon open to

news. They reportedly sent an emissary to the hospital to retrieve any valuable family jewellery on the body. They then ordered the hospital to embalm the body right away, thus making it impossible for a post-mortem to be carried out. In particular, it was not possible to ascertain whether the princess had been pregnant or not. (She had apparently confided to Doctor Mailliez that she was.) When the press learned of the tragedy, the royal family were roundly condemned for not issuing an official statement and for failing to fly the palace flags at half-mast.

To this day, new theories are still pointing to the possibility that the top ranks of the British establishment joined in a conspiracy to kill Diana, Princess of Wales, because she had not only become an embarrassment to the royal family but also to the state in general. Other theories have also emerged, one of which is that she faked her own death so that she could disappear, thus avoiding the media circus that followed her everywhere she went. Perhaps we will never know the full truth.

What is clear, though, is that the circumstances of her death were not as straightforward as they at first appeared. Also, many of those who dealt with the accident, whether in Britain or in France, were guilty of incompetence, if not murder. In 2005 the official enquiry into Diana's death has been reopened in France.

traffic once again. In normal circumstances, one would have expected the authorities to have sealed off the tunnel and have sifted through the evidence in order to find out exactly what had happened. But in this case they did not, which was curious.

THE AFTERMATH

Once Diana had died in hospital, the British royal family reacted oddly to the

THE JONESTOWN MASSACRE

Some events are so utterly bizarre and apparently inexplicable that conspiracy theories inevitably grow up around them, if only just to try and explain what on earth happened. One such event was the Jonestown Massacre, in which more than 900 people, all members of a cult living in a commune in Guyana, committed suicide by drinking Kool-aid laced with cyanide. Many of the dead were children who were given the lethal cocktail by their parents. Could it really be that they were all so much in awe of the cult leader, the Revd Jim Jones, that they willingly obeyed his order to commit suicide? Or were more sinister forces at work?

Before we can begin to answer that question we need to look at the facts of the matter. At the heart of whatever happened in Jonestown was the enigmatic figure of Jim Jones. Jones was born in Indiana in 1931. As a boy he became an avid member of a local Pentecostal church. By the time he was in his mid teens he had become a preacher, taking his message to the streets of

ABOVE: BODIES OF FOLLOWERS OF REVEREND JIM JONES LIE SPRAWLED IN DEATH ACROSS THE CULT'S COMPOUND IN GUYANA WHERE THEY COMMITTED A MASS SUICIDE BY DRINKING POISONED KOOL-AID.

Indianapolis, to both black and white communities. At the very beginning of his career his core values were apparently based around a sympathy with the underdog, regardless of race.

Nuclear war

Jones became a preacher at a Methodist Church in a white area and made a point of inviting black people to attend. By the late fifties he had his own church in Indianapolis, which he called The People's Temple. It ran programmes for the poor, including a soup kitchen, and his message of racial tolerance gained in popularity as the civil rights movement began to emerge. As he became increasingly critical of organized religion he moved closer to a kind of revolutionary socialism.

The prospect of nuclear war was also becoming a worry to Jones and he conceived the idea of moving his congregation abroad to somewhere that would be safe from nuclear attack. From 1963 to 1965 he travelled around looking for such a place, while assistants ran his church. He spent time in Hawaii and Brazil and then, on his way back to the United States, he visited the newly-socialist South American country of Guyana. Here, he thought, might be the perfect place for his new community.

Such a move would involve money that Jones did not yet have, so instead he moved his church to Ukiah, California, a place he believed to be relatively safe from nuclear attack. At first his church fared badly, with Jones himself becoming increasingly paranoid and dependent on prescription drugs. Following a link with a much larger organization, however, the Disciples Of Christ, his fortunes started to rise again. His following increased and he opened new churches in San Francisco and Los Angeles. Increasingly, his congregation was drawn from the poor black ghettoes. After Jones moved to San Francisco his church there was seen to be a real force for good and he became an influential political figure in the city during the early- to mid- 1970s.

The jungle Utopia

In 1973, Jones began work on building his long dreamed of community in the Guyanese jungle. He named it Jonestown in his own honour. When, in 1977, his church, now with some thousands of members, came under investigation for tax evasion he made the decision to move his whole operation to Jonestown.

Just fifty members of the Peoples' Temple moved to Jonestown at first but by late 1978 the population had risen to over 1,000. In the early days it seemed that this was a genuinely Utopian story. Here was an interracial community living in harmony and supporting itself by agriculture. Gradually, though, reports began to leak out that all was not as it seemed. An article in the *San Francisco Examiner* on 13 November 1977 related the story of one Bob Houston whose father believed that he had been murdered when he had attempted to leave the Temple. Claims started to emerge that people were being held against their will at Jonestown. A local congressman, Leo Ryan, became interested in this story, all the more so when, in June 1978, he heard the testimony of Debbie Blakey, a defector from the community, who claimed that Jim Jones had led the population in rehearsals for a mass suicide.

Ryan decided that he had to investigate these alarming claims. On 14 November 1978, he flew out to Guyana along with his staff, a number of journalists and some concerned relatives. After some resistance from Jones and his aides, Ryan was finally allowed to visit on the evening of Friday 17th. Jones made sure that the community put on a show of unity but during the visit messages were passed to Ryan and the other visitors from people in the community who were anxious to leave.

Ryan told Jones that some people wanted to leave and he appeared to be happy for them to go. On the next day Ryan led a party of around twenty defectors to the nearby airstrip of Port Kaituma. Two light aircraft were to meet them and take them back to the Guyanese capital of Georgetown.

ABOVE: DEAD CULT MEMBERS AMIDST THE DEBRIS OF POISON AND KOOL-AID CUPS USED TO ADMINSTER THE POISON.

CAMERAMAN FILMED HIS OWN MURDER

On reaching the airstrip, however, one of the apparent defectors, thought to have been planted by Jones, turned a gun on his fellow members and shot and killed two of them. Then a truck and a tractor belonging to the Temple arrived and several armed gunmen opened fire. Ryan was shot dead, along with another defector and three

ABOVE: REVEREND JIM JONES PREACHING FROM THE PULPIT OF THE PREACHER'S TEMPLE, INDIANAPOLIS.

journalists, including cameraman Robert Brown, who captured most of the awful events on film before being shot himself.

Meanwhile, back at the Jonestown compound, Jones had been tipped him over the edge by the defections, even though he had initially appeared to take the news calmly. He called a meeting of the entire population and told them that these desertions marked the end of their Utopia and that the only thing to do was commit suicide. The meeting was recorded on tape and, amazingly enough, it is clear that most of those present agreed with Jones. Some members suggested that the children should be allowed to live but Jones overruled them

and vats of poisoned soft drinks were brought out. The children were given their doses first: the poison was squirted into the mouths of the babies using syringes. The adults watched them die, then killed themselves.

Some did try to escape but they were faced with armed guards who shot at them. Many were killed, but over a hundred managed to escape into the jungle. Jim Jones himself died from a bullet in the head while sitting in his chair. It was presumably suicide. When outside helpers finally arrived they were greeted by a scene of unimaginable horror. Some 913 dead bodies lay there, many of them in orderly rows.

MIND CONTROL AND THE CIA

So was this simply an epidemic of madness – a classic story of a religious cult that had run out of control – or was there a hidden agenda behind the slaughter? It was not long before the first conspiracy theories appeared. The initial focus of suspicion, as is so often the case, was the CIA. Could Jonestown have been the site of a secret CIA mind-control programme that had just gone a bit too far? After all, the Jonestown settlement

WAS JONESTOWN THE SITE OF A SECRET CIA EXPERIMENT?

started up just as the CIA's notorious MKULTRA mind control programme was officially closed down. Could it have been revived illegally at Jonestown? The reason for the mass suicide, according to this theory, was that Leo Ryan had discovered the CIA's involvement during his visit and the mass suicide was staged to cover it up.

If that sounds breathtakingly cynical, it is nothing compared with the variant on this theory. This suggests that Leo Ryan was already on a CIA hit-list because of his sponsorship of the Hughes–Ryan Amendment which, if passed, would have required that the CIA report its planned covert missions to Congress for approval. According to this theory the real point of the events in Guyana was the murder of Leo Ryan – the mass suicide was simply staged in order to detract attention from this. However suspicious one might be of the CIA's involvement in covert activities though, the suggestion that they would be capable of murdering over 900 people in order to cover up the killing of a single man rather beggars belief.

In 1980, the House Permanent Select Committee on Intelligence investigated the Jonestown mass suicide and announced that there was no evidence of CIA involvement there. This, of course, failed to satisfy the conspiracy theorists and their case has been helped by the fact that the United States Government has consistently refused to release any of the classified papers relating to the case.

Is it likely that the CIA really were involved in this appalling event? Probably not – or at least not in any instrumental role. The tape of the last speech made by Jones and the testimony of the survivors (many of whom still believe that Jonestown was at first a positive community) suggests that what happened at the end was after all a kind of collective madness, rather than a plot with any rational intention behind it. In some ways, the idea that the mass suicide happened for a purpose, rather than as a result of deranged behaviour on a grand scale, may be easier for us to accept – which is why conspiracy theories concerning the Jonestown Massacre continue to abound.

JOHN LENNON AND THE FBI

When John Lennon was murdered on 8 December 1980, the world reeled in shock. At the time of his death, Lennon was one of the most famous rock stars of all time and after a quiet period away from the public eye he was in the process of returning to the limelight with his first album in five years.

He was shot outside the Dakota Building, where he lived, by a young man named Mark Chapman who was obsessed by his hero and who had a history of mental illness. When Lennon arrived at the building that day with Yoko Ono, Chapman raised a gun and shot the star four times as he tried to run away.

BELOW: JOHN LENNON POSES WITH FAN PAUL GORESH ON 8 DECEMBER, 1980. HOURS LATER, LENNON WOULD BE SHOT DEAD BY MARK CHAPMAN.

THE NEW STANDARD

Tuesday, December 9, 1980.   Price 12p

Incorporating the **Evening News**

CLOSING PRICES

John Lennon's last words

"HELP ME... I'VE BEEN SHOT'

YOKO ONO weeps as record producer David Geffen comforts her at the hospital.

from Nicky Holford
in New York

JOHN LENNON is dead. The former Beatle was murdered at 4 a.m. today outside his New York home by a crazed, smiling gunman.

Lennon, 40, was rushed to hospital in a police car but was dead on arrival.

Lennon and his wife, Yoko Ono, had just arrived home at the Dakota, luxury apartment building on Manhattan's Upper West Side, from a late-night recording session.

As they stepped out of their limousine they were accosted by the gunman and an argument broke out.

The man, who had earlier got Lennon to sign his latest album Double Fantasy—and had been seen lurking

In praise of John Lennon

John Blake, Maureen Cleave, Ray Connolly: Centre Pages

round the building for three days—pulled a .38 revolver from under his coat, crouched combat-style and fired five times.

Lennon staggered about five feet to a small guard's booth in the court-yard of the building.

Gasping "I am shot" repeatedly, he managed to climb six steps before collapsing face down in a pool of blood.

As he lay dying in his wife's arms, he softly whispered: "Help me."

"Do you know what you just did?" the doorman asked the man. "I just shot John Lennon," the gunman answered and threw down the gun.

Police spokesman Ed Burns said: "A police car was on the scene within minutes and he was rushed to hospital. But he died on the way."

Neighbour Carrie Rouse heard the gunfire and rushed across the road to see Lennon being cradled in his wife's arms. She heard his last words.

"It was only a whisper," she said. "But I heard him say: 'Help me.' Then Yoko screamed: 'He's been shot, he's been shot. Somebody come quickly.' She was hysterical.

Bleeding heavily

"He was bleeding heavily. His eyes were closed. Then he slowly rolled over."

Another witness, Sean Strube, said he had seen the man, who was wearing a tan overcoat and yellow tinted glasses, hanging around on the sidewalk all week and around the entrance of Lennon's apartment for hours that night.

"He had a smile on his face

Cont. Page 2, Col 1

JOHN LENNON: Help me

TV 27 • Entertainment Guide 29 • Commuter Club 11 • Ad Lib 20 • Compton Miller 22 • Patric Walker 28 • Delia Smith 31 • City 42

Lennon was rushed to hospital but died soon after his arrival. His death was mourned by thousands and he continues to be remembered by legions of fans.

The generally accepted view of the murder is that the mentally unstable Chapman acted alone, but there were also those who believed that Lennon was the victim of a conspiracy and that Chapman had in fact acted under orders from a higher authority.

"Dangerous extremists"
During the late 1960s and the early 1970s, John Lennon had become unpopular with the United States Government because of his outspoken criticism of the Vietnam war, among other issues. In a period when the counterculture was at its height, Lennon was seen as one of the most influential figures of the day and he was regarded by the government as highly subversive. J. Edgar Hoover of the FBI noted on Lennon's file that "all extremists should be considered dangerous".

As a result of the antagonism that arose between the star and the United States authorities, Lennon was denied permanent residency in America and the administration was constantly looking for ways to deport him. By 1972, Lennon was known to be under surveillance and it was reported that he had spoken about fearing for his life and that of his family. He

LEFT: THE DEATH OF JOHN LENNON AT THE HANDS OF CRAZED 'FAN' MARK CHAPMAN MARKED A NEW INTENSITY OF CELEBRITY OBSESSION. HERE THE LONDON *NEW STANDARD* REPORTS ON THE KILLING THAT SHOCKED THE WORLD.

continued to be monitored by the FBI even when he retired from public life altogether, although less consistently.

Under the Carter administration, the authorities began to take less interest in the politically inactive Lennon, but when President Reagan was elected in 1980 all that changed. It so happened that Lennon emerged from his seclusion just as the new, right-wing administration was beginning to step up its anti-extremist tactics. To some, the fact that Lennon was murdered just a few months after he stepped into the limelight once more was highly significant.

Hard evidence
Although it is undoubtedly true that Lennon and his wife Yoko Ono were under suspicion from the United States administration for many years, there is a lack of hard evidence to link Mark Chapman to the FBI and the CIA. Several authors have suggested that government agencies brainwashed the insecure and mentally fragile Chapman, conducting "mind control" programmes on him that ordered him to murder John Lennon. However, while there is plenty of documented evidence of Lennon's battle with the United States authorities in the shape of FBI files, those who claim that the government went one step further than mere harassment and had the star shot, using Chapman as the assassin, have very little in the way of facts to back them up. While the accounts of Lennon's constant run-ins with the authorities make

fascinating reading – for a time, he was friendly with many of the leading lights of the United States counterculture, such as Jerry Rubin and Abbie Hoffman – it is difficult to see why the government would choose to resolve the conflict by having Lennon murdered. Even if they did, why and how they would have used Chapman to do the deed is another question.

MIND CONTROL

Several commentators have speculated that Chapman was specifically programmed to kill on command. They point to "Project Bluebird" and "Project Artichoke", the CIA's attempts to investigate the possibilities of using scientific methods to control the behaviour of their agents. "Mind control" experiments were conducted using a number of methods including hypnosis and drugs. Chapman, it is alleged, became a pawn in this game, a "Manchurian Candidate" who was cold-bloodedly programmed to go out and shoot Lennon for the security services.

Whether or not a person can, in fact, be trained to kill – particularly if this is against their wishes – is questionable. On the other hand, some psychologists have argued that where a subject has a deep-seated desire to kill, and has a specific target in mind, he or she may be encouraged to do so by using various persuasive techniques. This is, of course, especially effective where a subject already has a distorted sense of reality, as in the case of Mark Chapman.

Conspiracy theorists argue that by using a lone drifter with a history of mental illness to commit the murder, the FBI would draw attention away from their own involvement in the crime. However, there are several problems with this theory, apart from the fact that there is so little hard evidence to support it. In particular, it seems unlikely that such a person would make a reliable hit man, to say the least. By the time of his death, John Lennon had made himself very unpopular with the powers that be, both as a result of his political pronouncements and his affiliations to left-wing groups. However, the idea that the CIA or the FBI decided to resolve the situation by programming a mentally unstable gunman to take potshots at him in the middle of New York does seem a little far-fetched.

The fact remains, though, that in 1980 John Lennon was re-emerging from a fallow period to become a public figure once again and that this coincided with a shift towards the right in American politics. Perhaps it was the case that the United States administration feared a re-run of the battles that Lennon had fought with the authorities in the past. Nevertheless, in the absence of hard evidence to link Chapman to the security agencies, it seems more likely that this was sheer coincidence and that, tragically, Lennon met his death just as his star was beginning to rise once more. Perhaps it is harder for many to accept that he was the unfortunate victim of a random killing than that there was a conspiracy to plot his murder.

THE SHOOTING OF TUPAC AND BIGGIE

During the early 1990s, rap became the biggest music in America and its leading artists not only started to appear in the pop charts but also in the news headlines. Increasingly, the new breed of rappers not only described the gangster life but they started to live it too. Two of the leading names in the world of gangster rap were Tupac Shakur and the Notorious B.I.G. (a.k.a. Christopher Wallace or Biggie Smalls).

Initially friends, they soon became sworn rivals. In fact, the two men seemed to be polar opposites. Tupac was based on the West coast while Biggie was based on the East. Tupac was signed to one leading rap label, Death Row, while Biggie was signed to its leading competitor, Bad Boy. Even their physiques were very different. Tupac was wiry and lean while Biggie, as his name suggests, was big all round. Both of them, however, were shot down in their prime, and the circumstances of their murders have kept the conspiracy theorists busy ever since.

Tupac was born in the Bronx, New York City on 16 June 1971. His given name was Lesane Parish Crooks but soon after his birth his mother Afeni, a member of the Black Panthers, changed his name to Tupac Amaru Shakur. He had a poverty-stricken, transient childhood in New York, before moving to Baltimore where he attended Baltimore School for the Arts

during his teens and studied dance and theatre. However, when the family moved again, this time to Marin County, California, Tupac started to go off the rails and became embroiled in drug dealing. He also started getting seriously involved in rap music, making his recording debut in 1990. In the following year his acting training paid off when he won a lead part in the gangster film *Juice*. In the same year, 1991, he also released his first album.

SHOT IN THE HEAD AND SURVIVED

All of a sudden Tupac was a star with a string of hit records and several more film appearances. At the same time, however, he became involved in a series of violent incidents. In one of these, in Oakland in 1991, Tupac was the victim of police brutality. In another he shot two policemen in Atlanta because he thought they were abusing a black motorist. Charges against Tupac were dropped, however, when the police officers were discovered to be intoxicated and in possession of stolen weapons. In December 1993 Tupac was charged with sexually abusing a woman in his hotel room and was subsequently sentenced to four years in prison. While still on remand, though, Tupac was shot five times by two men in a New York recording studio. He survived, despite being shot in the head and in a

ABOVE: RAP STAR NOTORIOUS B.I.G, AKA BIGGIE SMALLS, PICTURED HERE WITH LABEL BOSS SEAN 'PUFFY' COMBS. MANY BLAME SMALLS' SHOOTING ON THE INTENSE RIVALRY WHICH EXISTED BETWEEN THE EAST COAST AND WEST COAST RAP SCENES.

subsequent interview said that he believed that Biggie, who up until then he had considered a friend, and Biggie's label boss Sean "Puffy" Combs, were responsible for the attack.

In the following year, February 1995, Tupac began his prison sentence. He was released after eight months, when his own label boss Suge Knight put up $1.4 million bail. In return for this, however, Tupac had to agree to release three albums for Knight's Death Row Records.

The first of these albums, All Eyez on Me, sold more than nine million copies. Disturbingly, the video for the single "I Ain't Mad at Cha", filmed a month before his death, showed Tupac being shot and killed. Immediately before his death Tupac recorded another album, The Don Killuminati: The 7 Day Theory, using the pseudonym Makaveli.

A prophetic album

The album was full of death-related imagery and it soon proved prophetic. On 7 September 1996 Tupac Shakur was hit four times in a drive-by shooting in Las Vegas, after watching a boxing match between Mike Tyson and Bruce Seldon. He died from the four gunshot wounds in the Las Vegas University Medical Center hospital six days later, on February 13th.

The Las Vegas police never found the culprits but they believed that Tupac's killers were Southside Crips. The evidence for this was that a few hours earlier Tupac had been involved in a fight in a hotel lobby with a 21-year-old Crip named "Baby Lane" Anderson. Anderson was interviewed by the police but not charged with the murder. Witnesses, unsurprisingly, were reluctant to come forward.

Within the rap world, however, suspicion soon fell on Biggie Smalls and Bad Boy records. Rumours abounded that Biggie had paid the Crips to kill Tupac. Suspicion intensified when Tupac's friend, Yafeu "Kadafi" Fula, who had been present at the shooting and was believed to know the killer's identity, was himself killed in an execution-style murder in New Jersey.

While the rumours about Biggie's involvement were not enough to cause the police to act, it came as no surprise to the public when, on 9 March 1997, just two years after Tupac's murder, Biggie himself was gunned down in Los Angeles when leaving a party given by *Vibe* magazine. Once again, the police were unable to find

RUMOURS SOON BEGAN TO CIRCULATE TO THE EFFECT THAT BIGGIE HAD PAID THE SOUTHSIDE CRIPS TO KILL TUPAC.

ABOVE: RAPPER TUPAC SHAKUR ON STAGE. SHAKUR'S SHOOTING LEFT THE RAP WORLD SHOCKED: IT WOULD BE FAR FROM THE LAST KILLING, HOWEVER.

a witness who was prepared to come forward to identify the gunmen and the case remains unsolved. However, this time the suspicion fell upon Tupac's label boss Suge Knight.

So were the two fallen rappers simply victims of a gang culture that had run out of control or were their murders deliberately brought about by their rap music rivals? A story in the *Los Angeles Times* purported to prove that Biggie had

ordered Tupac's killing, paid the killers, and provided them with the gun. The writer even alleged that Biggie had been in Los Angeles at the time. He did not explain, however, that no one had noticed the presence of the 6ft 3in 300lb rapper and his entourage. And in due course, clear evidence was produced to demonstrate that Biggie had been in a New York recording studio at the time of Tupac's death.

ONE THEORY RUNS THAT TUPAC, LIKE ELVIS, FAKED HIS OWN DEATH: EVIDENCE CITED INCLUDES HIS RECORDING OF HIS FINAL ALBUM UNDER THE NAME 'MAKAVELI'.

WORTH MORE DEAD THAN ALIVE? Interest in the case was re-ignited in 2002 by the documentary Biggie and Tupac, made by British film-maker Nick Broomfield. The film pointed towards a sensational conclusion – that Suge Knight might have been responsible for murdering his own artist, Tupac, and that he then killed Biggie in order to cover up the initial murder so that it would look like a revenge killing.

The motive for this, supposedly, was that Tupac was about to leave Death Row having discovered that Knight was cheating him of royalties. At that point Knight decided Tupac was worth more to him dead than alive (a theory borne out by the enormous success of Tupac's posthumous releases). This idea was backed up by an alleged prison confession by Knight to another inmate and also by Knight's long record of using violence to get his own way in business deals.

It is a neat theory but one with a lot of holes in it. For starters, Knight was sitting next to Tupac when the car they were in was sprayed with bullets. One bullet nicked Knight's head. It would have been an incredibly risky plan for Knight to execute. Secondly, if the murder of Biggie was committed in order to cover up the killing of Tupac, surely he would have carried it out sooner and not waited for two years. Also, Knight would inevitably have been a suspect in Biggie's murder.

That said, it is a lot more plausible than the other conspiracy theory that surrounds the case, which suggests that Tupac, like Elvis, is not dead at all. The evidence for this supposition is a familiar mix of song lyrics that allegedly point to Tupac having faked his own death, the fact that his last album cover had a picture of himself being crucified (Jesus was resurrected after his crucifixion) and his use of the name 'Makaveli' for this last album. This was inspired by his reading of Machiavelli, who once wrote that faking one's death is a useful tactic for fooling one's enemies.

Fans have added on an ever more tenuous list of supposed clues to Tupac's 'faked' death. However, they have a hard time gainsaying the evidence to the contrary that was provided by the 1997 publication of a leaked photograph showing Tupac's badly damaged corpse lying on an autopsy table.

CHAPTER SEVEN:

A CURSORY GLANCE AT THE MAGAZINE AND NEWSPAPER
RACKS IN ANY NEWSAGENT'S SHOP WILL REVEAL TO
WHAT EXTENT THE MODERN MEDIA REVELS IN THE
DOINGS OF CELEBRITIES. THE DEGREE OF INTEREST IN

CELEBRITY INDISCRETIONS

THE LIVES OF THE RICH AND FAMOUS MAY BE
UNPRECENDENTED, BUT THE INTEREST ITSELF IS NOT, AS
THE CONSPIRACY THEORIES SURROUNDING THE

ELVIS LIVES

On 16 August 1977 Elvis Aron Presley was still the King of Rock and Roll, but he was a king whose crown was slipping. He was forty-two years old. He had not had a major hit in years.He was addicted to a whole range of pills, both legal and illegal, and he was grossly overweight. His recent Las Vegas shows had frequently been embarrassing, with Elvis incoherent and visibly confused. So when he was found dead, lying on his bathroom floor, on that August day, there was sadness in abundance but not a great deal of surprise. For the world at large, it was a simple story of American success and excess, the cautionary tale of a young man who had the world at his feet but ended up self-indulgently throwing his life away.

For his millions of devoted fans, however, his death was harder to swallow. Few of them wanted to hear the stream of sordid revelations that emerged in the cash-in books that were written by members of his entourage, let alone read the profoundly hostile biography written by Albert Goldman. Most simply preferred to listen to the records and forget the last tragic years of their hero's life. Others, though, refused to accept the seemingly obvious fact of his demise at all. Very soon the rumours began to spread that Elvis was alive, that he had faked his own death. So were these simply the delusions of the devoted, or could there be any substance to the stories?

THE WAX DUMMY

When we take a closer look at Elvis's death, the first mystery we encounter is the matter of the autopsy. Originally, the Shelby County Medical Examiner, Dr. Jerry Francisco, claimed that the autopsy indicated that Presley died of "cardiac arrhythmia", which he described as a "severely irregular heartbeat" and "just

LEFT: ELVIS ON STAGE: STILL TAKEN FROM THE FILM *ELVIS ON TOUR* 1972. FOR MANY ELVIS FANS, THE BELIEF THAT THEIR HERO IS STILL ALIVE IS AN ACT OF FAITH.

due to an overdose of drugs, out of sensitivity to the feelings of his family and friends.

A little mysterious maybe, but hardly sinister. Yet this confusion as to the precise cause of death may have been the seed that led to much wilder rumours. Before long fans were reporting sightings of Elvis. One man took a photograph of the pool-house at Graceland a few months after Elvis's funeral. On looking at it closely it became clear that a person looking a lot like Elvis was sitting inside the pool house. A record emerged by one Sivle Nora (Elvis Aron backwards) which sounded uncannily like Elvis. Fans noticed that Elvis's middle name was mis-spelled Aaron on his gravestone – could that be a sign that Elvis was not really in there at all?

But if it was not Elvis, then who was in the coffin? Fans came up with the answer to that too. The figure in the coffin was a wax model of Elvis. After all, funeral-goers had commented on the waxy appearance of the body and one had claimed that Elvis's sideburns were glued to his head. Before long it was being asserted that a Presley family member had bought a wax model of Elvis not long before his "death".

Conspiracy theorists also produced a whole range of answers to the question of what happened to Elvis after his fake death. A helicopter was allegedly seen in the area as he was apparently dying and it

another name for a form of heart attack". This was highly credible, given that Elvis was overweight and known to suffer from hypertension, but it failed to mention the presence of up to eleven different drugs (of the legal variety) in his bloodstream. Francisco later admitted that he had deliberately avoided mentioning the drugs, or the possibility that Elvis's death was

was thought that he was taken away at the last minute by air. There were also allegations that the mail consignment that Elvis had signed for that morning had just been part of a ruse. He had purportedly taken delivery of the wax dummy and then disappeared into the mail truck. Another claim was that a passenger calling himself Jon Burrows – a name that Elvis had often used to protect his privacy – was seen catching a plane to Buenos Aires just around the time that the "death" was discovered.

ELVIS – UNDERCOVER AGENT?

So perhaps Elvis is alive and well and living in Buenos Aires or Kalamazoo, as others have claimed. But why would this be ? What would have possessed him to fake his own death? There are two main theories here. The first is that Elvis simply could not take the stress of his celebrity any longer. He realized that his lifestyle was killing him and he decided to make a clean break with his past. The second is that Elvis had a secret role as an honorary drugs agent for Richard Nixon and he was now working undercover for the government, infiltrating the Mafia. Unfortunately he got too close to his targets and was discovered and as a result the FBI faked his death as a piece of old-fashioned witness protection.

It is here that the "Elvis is alive" theories, tenuous to say the least in their accumulation of circumstantial evidence, really fall apart. None of them seem remotely compelling. Far from hating his

fame and celebrity, Elvis positively revelled in it. As for the idea that he was an undercover crime buster, it is perhaps a more likely theory than he was abducted by aliens – but not much.

"Elvis Is Alive" conspiracy theories make entertaining reading – and they

provided one Gail Brewer-Giorgio with a major bestseller that was simply entitled *Is Elvis Alive?* – but this seems to be a clear case of wishful thinking getting a lot of mileage out of absolutely no hard evidence at all. Yes, it may be the case that Elvis's death was not the result of a

simple heart attack, but the chances of him making a comeback any time soon are – as his namesake Elvis Costello once sang – less than zero.

The Profumo Affair

In 1962, Britain was a country on the cusp of change. For the most part it was still locked in post-war austerity and presided over by an elderly and patrician Prime Minister in the shape of Harold Macmillan. The signs of change were starting to appear though. A group from Liverpool called The Beatles were about to release their first single, and the satirical TV show That Was The Week That Was was starting to poke fun at establishment figures, politicians and even the royal family. For the first time in the mass media age the British public was starting to suspect that its elected representatives might not be the respectable figures they seemed to be.

Then came the case that seemed to prove all their suspicions right, the biggest scandal Britain had seen since the war. It began with a rumour that a certain British politician had been sleeping with a woman who was also sleeping with a Russian naval attaché – who was presumed to be a spy. Gradually names were fitted in. The attaché was called Ivanov. The girl was a dancer and hostess named Christine Keeler. And the politician, sensationally, was the Minister for War, John Profumo, an up-and-coming star of the Conservative Party.

The rumours spread to the point at which questions were asked in the House of Commons. Profumo made the fatal mistake of issuing a categorical denial, telling the chamber: "Miss Keeler and I were on friendly terms. There was no impropriety whatsoever in my acquaintanceship with Miss Keeler." However, the rumours continued to spread and the newspapers soon discovered that there was plenty of fire to go with the smoke. Profumo held out for a while, but ten weeks later he appeared before MPs again to say "with deep remorse" that he had deceived Parliament because he wanted to protect his wife and family and he would resign.

The man in the mask

If Profumo thought that would be the end of the affair however, he was wrong. The press had tasted blood and they wanted more. The background to the Keeler/Profumo affair began to emerge. The two had been introduced by Dr Stephen Ward, a society osteopath. Keeler lived in Ward's flat, just one of a number of pretty girls he liked to surround himself with. Rumours began to circulate that Ward's flat was the scene of exotic sex parties that were attended by prominent society figures. Soon, a yet more outlandish rumour surfaced, that of the man in the mask. Apparently this masked man was a fixture at Ward's parties. He would serve the guests entirely naked, apart from a mask. Later he would be fed from a dog bowl. Feverish speculation suggested that the masked man might be yet another cabinet minister. Ward was also the link to Ivanov. Was Ward himself a spy? And if so, for which side?

ABOVE: 18 JUNE, 1963: FORMER BRITISH MINISTER OF WAR JOHN PROFUMO AND WIFE VALERIE HOBSON ARRIVE AT HOME SHORTLY AFTER PROFUMO RESIGNED HIS POSITION. PROFUMO ADMITTED HAVING AN AFFAIR WITH MODEL CHRISTINE KEELER.

Then, so the story went, a pimp named "Lucky" Gordon arrived at Ward's flat waving a gun and looking for Keeler, who was allegedly his former girlfriend. Keeler ran off into hiding. At this point the beleaguered establishment evidently decided that enough was enough. The story had rumbled on for too long. Stephen Ward was prosecuted for living off immoral earnings and effectively

running a brothel in his home. Two girls were described as "immoral earners" in the charge. They were Christine Keeler and her friend, a vivacious blonde named Mandy Rice Davies.

"HE WOULD, WOULDN'T HE!"
The trial of Stephen Ward attracted enormous publicity. Keeler denied the charges, saying that Ward did not use

ABOVE: MANDY RICE DAVIES AND CHRISTINE KEELER LEAVING THE OLD BAILEY IN LONDON AFTER THE FIRST DAY OF THE STEPHEN WARD TRIAL IN THE PROFUMO SCANDAL, JULY 1963.

women and sex for cash, but to gain influence among his peers. However, she did make a statement in which she said that Profumo gave her money "for her mother". More damningly, Mandy Rice Davies admitted having sex for money in Ward's flat. Rice Davies's performance in the witness box made her an instant celebrity. The prosecution alleged that she had received money from Lord Astor in return for sex. When she was told Lord Astor had denied ever sleeping with her, she uttered the immortal line: "Well, he would, wouldn't he?" She became an instant emblem of the new Britain, a country no longer in awe of its leaders.

The case against Ward looked strong but Ward committed suicide on the very last day of the trial, before the jury reached their verdict. Finally the Profumo affair was over and the man who knew its darkest secrets had gone to his grave. That did not

stop the conspiracy theorists, however. Controversy still rages as to whether Ward was an innocent dupe or an agent of British Intelligence who got in over his head and was murdered, with the killing being passed off as a suicide. In her own book on the subject, published in 2001, Christine Keeler made the allegation that Ward was in fact an agent of Russian intelligence and did indeed pass secrets on to Ivanov. However, she has provided nothing in the way of evidence to back this story up.

In conclusion, one might say that a conspiracy of sorts might have been hatched in order to make sure that Ward took all the blame, thus letting more important figures off the hook. However, in the end, the real importance of the Profumo Affair was that it was a watershed in British public life. To all intents and purposes the swinging sixties started here.

THE LINDBERGH KIDNAPPING

In 1932, Charles Lindbergh was one of the most famous men in America. Seven years previously he had been the first man to fly single-handed across the Atlantic. In recognition of his achievement he had been made Colonel and given the nickname "the Lone Eagle". A naturally shy man, he did not find fame easy and he had spent the last few years building a country estate for himself and his young family near Hopewell, New Jersey.

Because the new house was not quite finished, the Lindberghs were in the habit of just spending weekends there. During the week they lived at the family home of Charles's wife, Anne Morrow Lindbergh. On this occasion, however, they decided to stay an extra day at the new house. It was a fateful decision. On the night of March 1, Betty Gow, nurse to the couple's twenty-month-old son Charles A. Lindbergh Jr, entered the child's bedroom at 10 p.m. and discovered that he was missing.

After twenty-five minutes of frantic searching the caretaker, Ollie Whately, called the police. Charles Lindbergh himself went out into the grounds armed with his rifle, but he was unable to see any possible kidnappers. When the police came they found footprints, a carpenter's chisel and, a hundred yards away, a home-made ladder divided into three parts. Soon afterwards, Lindbergh noticed that a ransom note had been left in the child's bedroom. It demanded a $50,000 ransom and it appeared to have been written by a German speaker with poor English.

THE GO-BETWEEN

From the start, Lindbergh took over the investigation himself, assisted by his lawyers. The extent of his celebrity was such that the police allowed him to conduct the investigation as he pleased. Quickly deciding that organized crime was behind the kidnapping, he called in a sometime gangster called Morris Rosner and paid him to scout around his underworld contacts for leads. Not surprisingly, this approach proved fruitless.

A week after the kidnapping, a retired teacher from the Bronx by the name of John F. Condon wrote a letter to a newspaper offering to add his own life savings of $1,000 to the ransom money if

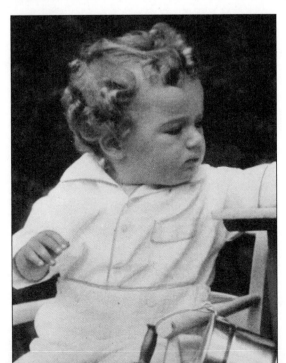

that would help persuade the kidnappers. Remarkably enough, Dr Condon soon received an approach from the kidnappers, who were using the same secret sign as that on the original ransom note. They asked him to become the go-between in the pay-off. Lindbergh agreed to this and before long Condon was contacted again and directed to a meeting with the presumed kidnapper in a cemetery. Condon nicknamed the man Cemetery John and said that the man had agreed to send him the child's sleep-suit as proof that he had the little boy. Once that was received, Condon was to hand over the full ransom.

The sleep-suit duly arrived in the post and on 2 April 1932 Lindbergh and Condon returned to the cemetery where Condon gave Cemetery John the $50,000 and received in return a letter which, the kidnapper said, would lead them to the boy. But the letter, mentioning a boat called the Nellie, laid a false trail. Cemetery John had escaped with the money and the Lindbergh baby was still missing.

A little over a month later, on May 2, the search finally came to an end. A truck driver discovered the decomposed body of an infant in woods two miles from the Lindbergh's house. After examining the infant's teeth Lindbergh announced that this was indeed his son. The child appeared to have died from a blow to the head, perhaps as the result of a fall. The kidnapping was now a murder investigation. However, the police still did not have any worthwhile leads and the trail grew cold. Two years later, however, a German-born carpenter called Bruno Richard Hauptmann was caught passing one of the bills from the ransom money. He had the same high cheekbones as Cemetery John but he was fair-haired and blue-eyed, unlike Condon's original description of the man. The police searched his house and found $18,000 of the ransom money hidden in his garage. Hauptmann was arrested and charged with the kidnapping and murder of the infant Charles.

SENSATIONAL TRIAL

The trial was a sensation. This was the beginning of the mass media age as radio carried news instantly across America. Apart from the fact that the money was found in his possession, most of the evidence against Hauptmann was either circumstantial or debatable. Lindbergh, for instance, claimed to identify his voice as that of Cemetery John, despite having only heard him utter six words two years previously. In the end though, the fact that he had the ransom money swayed the jury into finding him guilty of murder and he was sentenced to death by the electric chair. The sentence was finally carried out, after various appeals, on 3 April 1936.

No sooner had the guilty verdict been passed than rumours began to circulate that an innocent man had been convicted. According to the conspiracy theories that began to circulate, the real murderer could perhaps be found closer to home.

Two main alternative suspects have been suggested over the years. The first of these was Charles Lindbergh's sister-in-law, Elizabeth Morrow. Lindbergh had met the two Morrow sisters at the same time and had courted Elizabeth first before marrying Anne. According to this theory, Elizabeth had become pathologically jealous of her sister and of baby Charles. According to household sources, strict instructions had been issued to the effect that Elizabeth should never be left alone with the child. The conspiracy theorists suggested that Elizabeth must have evaded these strictures and murdered the baby in a fit of rage. There is no direct evidence of this state of affairs, of course, but it is true that Elizabeth was committed to a mental institution not long afterwards. The problem with this theory is that it would have been necessary for Charles Lindbergh and his wife, together with the entire domestic staff, to have been party to the conspiracy. Not only that, they would also need to have given false testimony at the trial, thus sending Hauptmann to his death. The theory is expounded at length in the book by Noel Behn, but it must be seen as speculative at best.

A CRUEL PRACTICAL JOKER

The second suspect is Charles Lindbergh himself, who was known for playing dangerous and cruel practical jokes. Once he planted a snake in a friend's bed. Another time, just weeks before the kidnapping, he hid the baby in a cupboard

and told his wife that it had gone missing. He kept the pretence up for a full half hour as his wife panicked.

So, according to this theory, Lindbergh may have carried out a prank that went disastrously wrong. Perhaps he climbed up the ladder himself in order to abduct his own son but dropped him as he attempted to leave, thus accidentally killing him. According to this theory he would then have faked the ransom note and conducted the investigation in a deliberate fashion.

Even if you find this rather outlandish scenario credible you may well wonder how Hauptmann fits into the story. The conspiracy theorists suggest that the whole ransom business was in fact unconnected with the actual kidnapping. It was just a group of criminals exploiting an opportunity for extortion, they suggest. According to this theory, although Hauptmann may have been an extortionist he was not a murderer.

There were certainly plenty of strange twists in the circumstances surrounding the case and Lindbergh's behaviour was no exception. On the other hand, one should keep in mind the fact that Lindbergh was not only reeling under the impact of celebrity but his child had also been abducted. He might well have been inclined to act strangely under those circumstances. However, despite all the anomalies, the jury's decision might have been the right one. This conclusion is reached by retired FBI man Jim Fisher, in his book on the subject.

Paul is Dead

By 1969 The Beatles were, in the words of John Lennon, "bigger than Jesus". They were internationally famous in a way that no pop group had ever been before. More than that, they were also the figureheads of a new generation. The 1960s had seen a rising generation question the old social certainties and The Beatles were among those at the forefront of this cultural revolution.

One result of this situation was that a lot of people started to take the work of The Beatles a lot more seriously then they should have done. People started to find all sorts of hidden meanings in their lyrics. One such disciple was Charles Manson, who believed that the White Album told him to send his followers out to murder Sharon Tate and her friends at their home in California.

Thankfully, such fanatical misreadings of the lyrics were confined to a tiny band of devotees. However, in 1969, a particularly strange Beatles rumour began to enjoy a wider circulation.

On 12 October 1969, disc jockey Russ Gibb, from Detroit's WKNR-FM, broadcast the extraordinary theory that Paul McCartney was dead, that he had been dead since 1966 and that he had been replaced by an impostor. The evidence, according to Gibb, was right in front of everyone. It was clearly audible in the

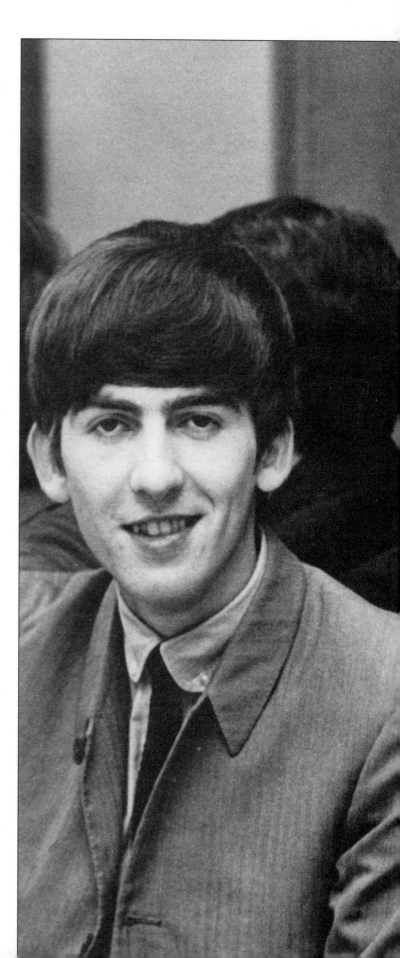

THE BEATLES (LEFT TO RIGHT): GEORGE HARRISON, PAUL McCARTNEY, JOHN LENNON, RINGO STARR. THE THEORY THAT PAUL McCARTNEY DIED IN 1966 WAS ONE THE GROUP THEMSELVES MAY HAVE ENCOURAGED.

CONSPIRACY THEORISTS CLAIM THAT PAUL MCCARTNEY WAS KILLED IN A CAR CRASH WHILE DISTRACTED BY A METER MAID (LOVELY RITA).

lyrics of the songs and it was visible on the record covers. Soon this rumour was sweeping the world, gaining new features with each retelling. However, most versions of the rumour shared these same essential features.

He blew his mind out in a car

What had happened, it was claimed, was that Paul McCartney was out driving when his attention was distracted by a traffic warden (Lovely Rita). He was involved in an appalling car crash in which he died, suffering terrible damage to his head. His body was so badly crushed that it was unidentifiable even from dental records. Because of the circumstances, the other Beatles were able to hush up Paul's death

while they decided how to keep the worlds' most popular band on the road. Soon they came up with a plan.

A Paul McCartney look-alike competition was announced. However, the winner's name was never announced because the lucky look-alike, William Campbell, had won a real prize – he was going to take over Paul's role in The Beatles. In order to further increase his resemblance to McCartney, Campbell underwent plastic surgery. However, the "new" Paul McCartney was not exactly identical to the old one, the conspiracy theorists argue. Campbell has a small scar over his upper lip and it is this that gives the game away.

What evidence is there for this outlandish theory? Well, almost all of it comes from the band's own work. After Paul's alleged death in November 1966, each album contained multiple clues as to his fate. Take Sgt. Pepper's Lonely Hearts Club Band, for instance. Here are just a few of the clues that have been spotted by the fans:

The cover photograph has the band standing by what appears to be a freshly dug grave.

The yellow flowers by the grave are in the shape of a bass guitar. Paul was the bass player for The Beatles.

There are three sticks on the yellow flowers to represent the three remaining Beatles.

Below the "T" in Beatles is a statue of the Hindu God Shiva, "The Destroyer". His hand points directly to Paul.

Paul is the only one holding a black instrument: another death association.

Turn to the lyrics and we hear "He blew his mind out in a car, he didn't notice that the lights had changed", from "A Day In The Life" and "Nothing to do to save his life", from "Good Morning Good Morning".

However, the real motherlode of clues can be found in the White Album. The words "number nine, number nine" on the track "Revolution 9" become "turn me on, dead man, turn me on, dead man" when played backwards. The track also includes other clues, such as the sound of a car crashing. A similar reversal at the end of "I'm So Tired" reveals "Paul is dead, man, miss him, miss him...". Another track, "Don't Pass Me By", has lyrics that read, "I'm sorry that I doubted you...I was so unfair. You were in a car crash, and you lost your hair...".

THE FUNERAL PROCESSION

There are fewer visual clues to Paul's alleged death in the White Album but the ultimate source for the conspiracy theorists – and the immediate inspiration for the original radio broadcasts – was 1969's Abbey Road album. It is alleged that the front cover of this album depicts Paul's funeral procession. The four Beatles are pictured crossing the road. Lennon is the clergyman or priest (dressed in white),

Starr is the funeral director or pallbearer (formally dressed), McCartney is the the corpse (he is out of step with the others and he has bare feet and a cigarette, which is a Sicilian symbol of death) and Harrison is the grave-digger (denim working clothes).

Furthermore, the license plate of the white car reads LMW 281F. LMW is said to stand for "Linda McCartney Widow (or Weeps)", and 28IF suggests that Paul would have been twenty-eight years old if he had not died. (At the time of the album's release, 26 September 1969, McCartney was in fact twenty-seven years old.) Additionally, the cigarette in the picture is in McCartney's right hand, even though he is left-handed.

In fact there appear to be so many clues, not to mention the dozens of photographs that allegedly prove that the later Paul McCartney is a different person to the original that, after a while, one can easily think that there must be something to it all. However, the fact that this new Paul McCartney look-alike went on to duplicate his hero's voice and his songwriting ability exposed the theory as the enjoyable nonsense that it plainly is.

Even The Beatles themselves saw the funny side of it. John Lennon, in the anti-Paul song "How Do You Sleep At Night?" from his solo album Imagine, includes the line "those freaks was right when they said you was dead". And, in 1993, McCartney himself paid tribute to this long-running conspiracy theory by calling his live album – what else? – Paul Is Live!

BIBLIOGRAPHY

GENERAL

Stewart Galanor, *Cover-Up*, Kestrel, 1998.

Devon Jackson, *Conspiranoia! The Mother of All Conspiracy Theories*, Penguin, 2000.

Michael Newton, *The Encyclopedia of Conspiracies and Conspiracy Theories*, Checkmark, 2005.

Jonathan Vankin and John Walen, *Eighty Greatest Conspiracies of All Time: History's Biggest Mysteries, Cover-ups and Cabals*, Citadel Press 2004.

http://www.alternet.org/story/148 73 Overview of current conspiracy theories.

http://www.carpenoctem.tv/ Useful site that includes a review of the most popular conspiracy theories to date.

http://www.coverups.com Entertaining site about the great cover-ups of history.

CHAPTER ONE: THE WAR ON TERROR

Jim Marrs, *Inside Job: Unmasking the 9/11 Conspiracies*, Origin, 2004.

John K. Cooley, *Unholy Wars: Afghanistan, America, and International Terrorism*, Pluto, 2002.

Robert Parry, *Secrecy & Privilege: Rise of the Bush Dynasty from Watergate to Iraq*, The Media Consortium, 2004.

CHAPTER TWO: SECRET SOCIETIES

http://www.conspiracyarchive.com Material on the Illuminati, secret societies, mind control, etc.

CHAPTER THREE: THE UNKNOWN

http://www.crystalinks.com/new mexico.html Information about the Roswell, New Mexico UFO/alien incident.

http://www.ufoevidence.org Site dedicated to UFO sightings, research, etc.

www.badastronomy.com For a sceptical, scientific view of conspiracy theories involving the moon landings, UFOs, etc, this site is hard to beat.

http://www.forteantimes.com Well-presented magazine concerning supernatural phenomena.

CHAPTER FOUR: WAR STORIES

Joachim C. Fest, *Inside Hitler's Bunker: the Last Days of the Third Reich*, Farrar, Straus and Giroux, 2004.

Richard J Evans, *Telling Lies About Hitler: The Holocaust, Hitler, and the David Irving Libel Trial*, Verso, 2002

Michael Shermer, *Why People Believe Weird Things, Pseudoscience, Superstition and Other Confusions of Our Time*, Owl Books, 2002

Michael Shermer & Alex Grobman, *Denying History: Who Says the Holocaust Never Happened, and Why Do They Say It?*, University of California Press, 2002

CHAPTER FIVE: POLITICAL COVER-UPS

Dick J. Reavis, *The Ashes of Waco: An Investigation*, Syracuse University Press, 1998.

Alexander Cockburn, Jeffrey St. Clair, *Whiteout: The CIA, Drugs and the Press*, Verso 1998.

CHAPTER SIX: MURDER MYSTERIES

James H. Fetzer (ed.), *Murder in Dealey Plaza: What We Know Now That We Didn't Know Then*, Open Court, 2000.

Noel Botham, *The Murder of Princess Diana*, Kensington Publishing Corporation, 2004.

Barbara Leaming, *Marilyn Monroe*, Three Rivers Press, 2000.

CHAPTER SEVEN: CELEBRITY INDISCRETIONS

Lloyd C. Gardner, *The Case That Never Dies: The Lindbergh Kidnapping*, Rutgers University Press, 2004

Matthew Parris & Kevin Maguire, *Great Parliamentary Scandals: Five Centuries of Calumny, Smear and Innnuendo*, Robson Books, 2004

Gail Brewer-Giorgio, *Is Elvis Alive?*, Tudor, 1988

Albert Goldman, *Elvis*, Penguin Books, 1982

Andru J Reeve, *Turn Me On, Dead Man: The Beatles and the 'Paul-Is-Dead' Hoax*, Authorhouse, 2004

INDEX